PRAISE

INSIDE THE EMPIRE

A *NEW YORK TIMES* BESTSELLER

"*Inside the Empire* gives baseball fans a rare, behind-the-scenes look at the 2018 New York Yankees season. But more than just a clubhouse diary, the book is dead-on in its depiction of a general manager's daily life and the many decisions that go into building a playoff team. Bob Klapisch and Paul Solotaroff's combined experience and engaging writing style make this book a fantastic read for anyone who follows the game."

— **Billy Beane, executive vice president of baseball operations, Oakland Athletics**

"Fans might think they are knowledgeable about the Yankees players, field staff, and front office. But *Inside the Empire* takes readers to another level — behind the scenes in the clubhouse and executive suites. It's entertaining, riveting, and totally enlightening. Couldn't put it down."

— **Ken Rosenthal, Insider at *The Athletic*, FOX Sports, MLB Network**

"The caps and jerseys never change, but these aren't the same old Yankees. With unprecedented access and penetrating insights, *Inside the Empire* illuminates the reimagined Bronx Bombers — Brian Cashman's smarter, sleeker operation that just might dominate the game, if only the hated Red Sox didn't do it even better. You might think you know these Yankees, but with Bob Klapisch and Paul Solotaroff as your tour guides, you're in for a lot of surprises, and a rollicking fun read."

— **Tyler Kepner, national baseball writer for the *New York Times***

"*Inside the Empire* is so much more than a baseball story. It burrows deep into the DNA of the most iconic team in American sports and offers an unsparing portrait of the New York Yankees and their delicate balance between moneyed monolith and quintessential modern organization. Bob Klapisch and Paul Solotaroff marry access, insight, and humor with a critical eye that reveals a never-before-seen side of a franchise in the midst of sweeping changes."

— Jeff Passan, ESPN Insider and
best-selling author of *The Arm*

"*Inside the Empire* pops open the hood of how the Yankees are run and gives us a rare peek at the machinery."

— Tom Verducci, *New York Times* best-selling author

"The first must-read of the baseball season. Some excellent behind-the-scenes reporting from cover to cover."

— Mike Vaccaro, *New York Post*

INSIDE THE EMPIRE

INSIDE THE EMPIRE

*The True Power
Behind the New York Yankees*

Bob Klapisch and Paul Solotaroff

Mariner Books
Houghton Mifflin Harcourt
Boston   New York

First Mariner Books edition 2020

Copyright © 2019 by Bob Klapisch and Paul Solotaroff

Photographs copyright © 2018 by Anthony J. Causi

For information about permission to reproduce selections from this book,
write to trade.permissions@hmhco.com or to Permissions,
Houghton Mifflin Harcourt Publishing Company, 3 Park Avenue,
19th Floor, New York, New York 10016.

hmhbooks.com

Library of Congress Cataloging-in-Publication Data
Names: Klapisch, Bob, author. | Solotaroff, Paul, author.
Title: Inside the empire : the true power behind the New York Yankees /
Bob Klapisch and Paul Solotaroff.
Description: Boston : Houghton Mifflin Harcourt, 2019. |
Includes bibliographical references and index.
Identifiers: LCCN 2018057177 (print) | LCCN 2018060027 (ebook) |
ISBN 9781328589125 (ebook) | ISBN 9781328589354 (hardcover) |
ISBN 9780358299240 (paperback)
Subjects: LCSH: New York Yankees (Baseball team) — Management — History.
Classification: LCC GV875.N4 (ebook) | LCC GV875.N4 K53 2019 (print) |
DDC 796.357/64097471 — dc23
LC record available at https://lccn.loc.gov/2018057177

Book design by Chloe Foster

Printed in the United States of America
DOC 10 9 8 7 6 5 4 3 2 1

To the crew at Casa Klapisch: Kristy, Casey, Kaley, and Corky

— Bob Klapisch

For CC and Luke, who light the path and keep me firmly to it

— Paul Solotaroff

Contents

INSIDE THE EMPIRE

1

LOCKED AND LOADED:
WELCOME TO THE BRONX POWER STATION

The General Manager Meetings each fall are baseball's version of a buddies' fishing junket to Belize. Executives harrowed by the grind of the season — six months of seven-day/eighty-hour weeks; back-page eruptions after three-game slumps; and side-eyed shade from their high school daughters over *another* pre-prom party not attended — disappear for four days in mid-November to a luxe hotel overlooking a golf course.

None of the GMs can putt worth a damn, but the greens are beside the point. Their fixed destination is the lobby bar, where someone's playing piano, the shades are drawn against the late-fall sun, and thirty men with the hardest jobs in the trade can let loose and get buzzed. Each man has his clique of whiskey pals — the ones he met while working his way up the organizational chart of his club, or the two or three peers he's grown comfortable making deals with since he ascended the throne. Not a lot gets done at these boys'-club excursions, in part because of the calendar. The free-agent market is barely a week old, no one's finalized his forty-man roster, and the needs of each team won't fully manifest until the frenzy of Winter Meetings one month hence. *Those* events, held in mid-December at another Kubla Khan luxe resort, are a Ford Bronco chase of trades and desperation, capitalism on a four-day crack toot.

In addition, supplicants by the thousands show up to try to make their luck there: vendors, beat writers, unemployed scouts and coaches, and moon-eyed fans and their kids. Such is the noise and traffic that GMs hole up in their suites, texting each other madly to find a right-handed bat or a couple of young pitchers with controllable years. The stakes couldn't be higher for those concerned. Any executive who goes home empty this year may be back at next year's Winter Meetings looking for work.

Still, it's not like *nothing* happens at the GM meetings one month prior. Over third and fourth cocktails, GMs pull each other's strings for leads on what they hope they'll get done later. At one point or another, most will pay homage to the guy or two holding all the cards: the lucky executives who happen to have deep wells of talent on their Double- and Triple-A rosters. In this, the Age of the Real-Deal Drug Test and the Can't-Miss Hall of Famer Clogging the Lineup, nobody wants the fading superstar with the enormous contract. What the GMs want — overwhelmingly — is to get younger and cheaper: to trade a couple of peak seasons from their franchise left fielder for a pair of live-armed kids who are on the brink.

It was precisely in that spirit of here-goes-nothing that Mike Hill, the director of baseball operations for the fire-sale Miami Marlins, tapped Brian Cashman on the shoulder in November 2017 in the hallway of the Waldorf Astoria in Orlando. After fifteen years of being a reluctant shopper — the one guy who showed up *every* winter with strict orders to overpay for back-nine players — Cashman, the general manager of the New York Yankees, was suddenly in the catbird seat. Through a series of canny drafts and quick-strike deals at the trading deadline a year or so back, he'd miraculously recast himself as a master builder, the cool kid with all the hot toys. He had seven of the hundred best prospects in the game (plus a wave of kids behind them who were almost as good) and a major league roster of newly minted mashers who'd bulled their way to within a game of the World Series.

Cashman also had the one great luxury in the room: permission to do *absolutely nothing*. His Baby Bombers had come of age two years early and bought him a full season to sit tight. With a mix of pending superstars on minimum-salary deals (Aaron Judge, Gary Sánchez, Luis Severino), cut-rate acquisitions on the cusp of stardom (Didi Gregorius, Chad Green, Sonny Gray), and just the right garnish of graybeard leaders to run the locker room (Brett Gardner, CC Sabathia, David Robertson), he could bide his time for the auction to end all auctions: the 2019 free-agent class. Come November of the following year, he'd have a hundred million or more in luxury cap space to add the keystone blocks for a five-year run: perhaps Bryce Harper to bang dents in the second-deck facade, Manny Machado to anchor a world-class infield, or Clayton Kershaw to start Game 1 of the World Series.

Still, you know: it never hurts to talk. "We were walking down the hall when either Hill or I broached the subject of Stanton," Cashman says. Giancarlo Stanton was the circus-strongman slugger who'd pummeled the National League for eight years. Fresh off a fifty-nine-home-run season and a Most Valuable Player Award in 2017, he was a wild extravagance on the now-threadbare Marlins, a Ferrari at a drive-in showing *The Florida Project*. The Marlins franchise (and its many hundreds of millions in debt) had been sold months before, for $1.2 billion, to a baggy-suited rich guy by the name of Bruce Sherman and his new partner, Derek Jeter. Of the several entities that pursued the Marlins (among them, a consortium headed by Jeb Bush and another by Jared Kushner's father, Charles), the Sherman-Jeter group seemed the least provisioned to ride out years of heavy losses. Sherman had walked away from Private Capital Management, his wealth management firm, after a string of big bets blew up in his face. Among them were sunk positions in Bear Stearns, the Great Crash failure, and newspaper chains like Knight Ridder and Gannett that chunked off billions of dollars in high-speed losses. Over four years' time, PCM's portfolio shrank by 90 percent. To be sure, Sherman owned a $70 million yacht, which he had humbly christened *The Majestic,* and he'd deftly repotted himself in old-growth Naples, where he chaired a wine festival every winter. But in team-owner waters, he was plankton to sharks, a multimillionaire in a billionaire boys' club.

The Sherman-Jeter purchase of the Marlins was predicated on a promise that they'd made to the other owners in the game: that they'd instantly strip the team of homegrown stars and slash its obligations to the bone. Having overshot the market by about $200 million — their chief rival, a construction magnate named Jorge Mas, had stopped bidding at $1 billion — they told their fellow owners that they'd go the Houston Astros route: tank for four years while turning a modest profit and building back a core of young talent.

But it's hard to make a buck by wooing pissed-off fans, then playing them for suckers two months later. Pre-sale, Sherman and Jeter advertised a team built around assets like Stanton. After the deal closed, though, word leaked to the *Miami Herald* about a secret prospectus given to investors. It talked up scorched-earth payrolls, absurdly robust gate sales, and cash infusions from a phantom TV deal. This, after Jeter and Sherman botched the takeover by firing goodwill legends like Andre Dawson and Jeff Conine and dumping a longtime scout with colon cancer. As southern rollouts go, this was William Tecumseh Sherman burning down Atlanta. At a town hall meeting to assuage hurt feelings, Jeter kiddingly told a fan that he could throw out the first pitch, as long as he bought a ten-year ticket plan.

The first big name Jeter put on the block? Giancarlo Stanton. Stanton, among the highest-paid position players in baseball, had ten years left on a thirteen-year deal worth $325 million. Alas for Jeter, Stanton also had leverage — veto rights over any proposed trade. For eight years, he'd played the good-egg soldier, hacking ninety-loss seasons in 100-degree heat to stand sweat-soaked and disheartened in right field. As his agent, Joel Wolfe, told *USA Today,* "he spends Octobers in Europe, unable to watch the playoffs because it kills him." Now he'd earned the right to go to a sure winner: a team with deep pockets, a stocked pond of talent, and the guts to push all in for five years. Effectively, that ruled out all but four teams: the Yankees, Dodgers, Cubs, and Astros. Not for Stanton the midmarket clubs riding a short wave up — the Clevelands and Colorados with a three-year window if *everything* broke in their favor. And no as well to longtime contenders who'd come to the end of their run — the San Francisco Giants and St. Louis Cardinals. If Jeter, the team president, wanted Stanton to expand his list, he was going to have to do some high-class groveling with his franchise player. And *that,* thought anyone who'd ever met Jeter, would be must-watch entertainment through Thanksgiving.

The courtship of a dejected superstar is one of the hardest dances in sports. Done right, it's a whisper-quiet, three-step waltz among the GM, the player, and his agent. "I'll give you an example," says Cashman, a disciplined cardsharp whose default face is a neutral stare. "Last winter, when I was dealing with Brian McCann, I called his agent [B. B. Abbott] to set the stage." McCann, a slugging catcher with a no-trade clause in his five-year, $85 million deal, had been ousted from his spot by Gary Sánchez, the first of the Baby Bombers to arrive. "I told [Abbott] to tell Mac, 'There's a place on this team for you. You can be the backup and we'll have the DH open, so if you're cool with that, then we're good. But if you want me to [talk] trades, I'm not going to disrespect you. You've earned the right to go where you like, so let me know what you want.'" Abbott talked to his client and got back to Cashman fast. "He said, 'We appreciate you handling it this way, Cash. But hey, on the down-low, Mac's not going anywhere west.'"

The Seattle Mariners were interested, but Cashman knew now not to engage them: the Braves and Astros were the only teams for whom McCann would waive his no-trade. Ever so softly, Cashman struck a deal with Houston: McCann (and most of his salary) for two green but electric starters pitching at the Single-A level. Both sides came up winners in the exchange — McCann earned a World Series ring in Houston, and Cashman moved most of his salary and used one of those kid pitchers in the trade he'd make for Stanton. His masterstroke: no one in the New York media got wind of the trade until it was almost done. "The last thing you want is Mac to hear from the papers, 'the Yankees are shopping you,'" says Cashman. Then the "writers call and commentate on the deal, and suddenly, you've got choppy waters." Instead, McCann left "throwing bouquets our way," glad for the chance to have been a Yankee.

Cashman, sitting at a Galleria lunch spot that passes for pan-Asian in Tampa, is a short, pale fellow with surprisingly broad shoulders and a thrumming disinterest in small talk. There is, in the fixity of his gaze and jawline, the set of a man taken lightly for too long. He's one of those people who came to power fairly, on the strength of his smarts and sweat equity. To be sure, he used a family connection to land an internship with the Yanks while in college. But from the moment he got his foot in the door, there was no stopping Cashman on the come-up. He was a baseball gym rat in college: too small to play for a prime-time program, he started all four years at Catholic University as its leadoff hitter and second baseman. He broke the school's record for hits in a season and batted .348 his junior year. Not bad for a guy who stood five-seven and swung at every first strike. "The first pitch of the game was almost always a fastball — that's why my average was so high," he says. "I took advantage of what I knew was coming."

Perhaps because he speaks in a colorless burr and likes the back of the pressroom, not the front, he's long been viewed as a kind of permanent temp, a substitute teacher who stuck around. For years, New York mistook him for an errand boy, the sad-eyed apparatchik catching hell from George Steinbrenner after a meaningless loss in April. He was paid less money than most of his peers, had smart trades sabotaged by The Boss, and appeared to survive where his forebears hadn't because he didn't punch back when abused. That last part was false, but he never troubled to correct it. "He and George would have scream festivals for *hours*," says Jean Afterman, the assistant GM of the Yankees, whose office at the new Stadium is next to Cashman's. "I'd close my door but could hear them down the hall. Brian backs down from no one — that's why George loved him."

Cashman, like the three or four masters of his craft, is one part diplomat to two parts pickpocket. He can politely boost your watch and wallet and leave you thinking the heist was your idea. Jeter's style, by contrast, is to dictate terms and expect you to glumly accept them. His first act after buying the Marlins was to pointlessly freeze out Stanton. He didn't book the obligatory get-to-know-you dinner with his star at a stuffy rooftop steakhouse in Miami. He declined to call Stanton and offer congratulations when he was named the league MVP. And he never phoned Wolfe, one of the powerhouse reps in baseball, to ask about his client's choice of destinations. "I was ready for the worst, which it was," Stanton confided, looming at his locker in a pair of gold spikes after a workout in spring training in 2018. Like Judge, Stanton is one of those physical freaks you can't properly appreciate on TV. It isn't only his mass or stone-cut proportions, but the taper of chest and back to a tiny waist. There's a quality about him that you sometimes find in art: grace and violence merged in random gestures. "If that's how you want to treat someone, then there's no playing nice," he said of Jeter. "I had had more than enough."

In late November 2017, he'd been given a *diktat* by Jeter. "It was, 'Take this fucking deal with the Giants or the Cardinals, or I promise you I'm trading everybody around you and you'll be stuck here forever,'" said someone who was privy to those talks. Stanton had seventy-two hours to agree. He didn't, per our sources, need them. Replying through his agent, he was River Avenue terse: *No, and HELL no, goddamnit.*

A thousand miles north, the Yankees looked on, appalled. "Derek's done a good job of pissing *everyone* off," said a member of the team's administration. "I'm sure the guys at MLB now are scratching their heads, thinking, 'What the fuck did we do by selecting him?'" Perhaps they looked at Jeter and mistook him for Magic Johnson, a hug-and-handshake natural who draws investors in droves and grows the worth of everything he touches. Instead, baseball's bosses got a celebrity who didn't seem to understand how relationships work at the executive level. "The press asked if Jeter felt the need to talk to Stanton, and he said, 'No, that's what my GM's for,'" said the Yankee staffer.

While Cashman insists that he liked Jeter as a player, it isn't entirely clear that he means it. Or maybe it's fairer to say that there were two Derek Jeters — the happy-go-lucky kid from Kalamazoo who came up at twenty-one and seduced the sport with his cool-hand poise, that gift for the big play on the grand stage, and the thirty-something Jeter who became somewhat hardened by fame. Treated like a civic institution in New York — worshiped by the faithful in their Jumpman-branded garb, teenage fan-girls rocking RE2PECT tank tops, and adored and protected by the tabloid scolds who trolled other stars on *Page Six* — he somehow remembered every slight and provocation. Jeter grew distant from writers who dared to notice that he couldn't get around on a good fastball. His initial coldness toward Alex Rodríguez was as stark as it was cruel: there was that graceless moment in 2006 when a routine pop fly somehow fell between them. Jeter, hands on hips, glared daggers at A-Rod, emasculating him on national TV. *That* Derek Jeter wasn't fun to general-manage — or to have playing behind you when you pitched. "When Andy [Pettitte] came back from Houston, there was a ground ball up the middle, and Andy's like, 'All right, that's an out,'" says Cashman. "Next thing you know, it goes through for a hit and he's like, 'Crap, Jetes can't get to those anymore.'"

Nonetheless, Jeter wanted to get paid like the player he'd been in his middle twenties. In the fall of 2010, he became a first-time free agent at the age of thirty-six. He'd had a bad year at the plate and a worse one in the field, but he demanded a max contract into his forties. Cashman pushed back, declining to bargain against himself. The terms he set and stuck to — $51 million for three years — pricked Jeter's damaged pride. "Jetes sent messages through his agent that we were fucking him when no one was willing to pay what we offered," says Cashman. "I'm like, 'How much higher do we have to be than *highest*?'" He invited Jeter and his agent, Casey Close, to go out and shop the deal. Jeter returned to the table smarting; no one had come close to the Yankees' bid. Close even suggested a stark concession for his client: a piece of either the YES Network or the team. "At the meeting, Derek said, 'What other short-stop would you want playing here?' and I started rolling off names," says Cashman. "I got, like, three names down and Casey said, 'Stop, this isn't productive.' Then Derek got up and goes, 'You guys finish this! I don't want to go anywhere else, but I don't want to be in here either!'"

For eight years, Cashman has staged a counterintuitive ritual. Each December, the normally cautious GM rappels down the face of a steel-and-glass tower to help launch Christmas season in Stamford, Connecticut. Dressed in a preposterous elf hat and gloves, he'd just descended the Landmark Building when he heard that Shohei Ohtani — a pitching/slugging phenomenon who was the purported Babe Ruth of Japan — had crossed the Yankees off the list of teams he would sign to play for this season. "He was our target, like every team in baseball: big arm and could really swing the bat," says Cashman. (With a pedigree for luring Japanese stars — Hideki Matsui and Masahiro Tanaka, just for starters — the Yankees had been clear favorites to get Ohtani.) Though he was under no pressure to devise a plan B, Cashman harked back to his chat about Stanton at the GM meetings. "I'd left the conversation with Hill at, 'Hey, I like your asset — this could play in the event we don't land Ohtani.'"

Till then, he'd really spent no time conceiving a Judge-and-Stanton lineup. Cashman is a grinder who prefers the hedged gamble to the high-risk, high-reward plunge. His best trades have always been for players on the come, or for someone's distressed asset at cost — a Didi Gregorius *before* he hit left-handers, a David Justice instead of Sammy Sosa. But in the weeks since he'd spoken to Hill in Orlando, the Marlins, meaning Jeter, had mucked things up. Word leaked out that their ultimatum with Stanton had failed, leaving them stuck with the slugger and his monstrous contract. Worse, none of the teams on Stanton's wish list would bite, even at a heady discount. The Marlins were going to have to *pay* someone to take their franchise star — to actually attach a fat check to offset his salary.

Cashman tasked his war team — Tim Naehring, vice president of baseball operations; Mike Fishman, the assistant general manager and director of the Analytics Department; and Afterman, the vice president in charge of contracts — to run the cost-benefit splits. Then he texted Hill, knowing not to call Jeter. "He wasn't interested in speaking, which, you know, whatever," says Cashman. At some point, Jeter realized that he'd nowhere else to turn and delegated the job to Hill. "Which is fine," says Cashman. "I like Michael a lot. He's a guy I've done deals with before."

That week, the one leading up to the 2017 Winter Meetings, Hill and Cashman volleyed texts, knocking names and numbers back and forth.

(Almost no one actually *speaks* now when making a trade. Cashman, a stickler for returning calls — it's one of the traits that endears him to his peers — says type is better than talk as deals evolve. There's no heat-of-battle tension in five-word squibs.) Hill started out by asking for the moon. He wanted a haul that began with Gleyber Torres, the Yanks' best prospect, and also included their Single-A phenom Estevan Florial. Cashman countered with third-tier kids and insisted that Hill take a veteran back — he'd never get sign-off from owner Hal Steinbrenner if he didn't move some money to offset Stanton's. For forty-eight hours, his hopes rose and sank; at least twice, Cashman thought he'd missed his chance. The Marlins put out word that they had heat with other teams, though Cashman's contacts at the MLB office told him it was just smoke, not fire.

On December 8, Cashman left the Stadium late, no surer of his footing than he'd been that morning. Earlier in the day, he thought he'd struck a deal, trading two young pitchers and the veteran Chase Headley for Stanton and $30 million in deferred cash. Things were far enough along that Cashman made two calls. One was to Hal Steinbrenner, the general partner of the Yankees and a man wired more like Cashman than his father. After years of acquiescing to the Big Stein template — wooing All-Star free agents and wildly overpaying them to placate fans and keep the Stadium full — Hal had come around to Cashman's view that you couldn't mortgage a championship anymore. It had worked for them once, in the winter of '08, when Hal spent almost half a billion dollars to win the '09 World Series and to baptize the new Yankee Stadium. But every max contract is a devil's bargain: what you get from a star on the front side of his deal will cost you, in spades, later on. By 2012, the players he'd signed for vast sums — CC Sabathia, Mark Teixeira, and A. J. Burnett — were sucking air, and Burnett had tanked so badly that the Yankees paid the Pirates to take him off their hands.

Still, your dear-bought habit is harder to break than the one that costs you nothing. In 2014, Hal splurged again on a haul of top free agents. *That* group, anonymous and painfully dull, never made it as far as the Division Series. It was out of their failure that a new way was born, a thorough reinvention of team culture. Mark Newman, the farm director and a George Steinbrenner holdover, was not so gently prodded to retire. His successor, Gary Denbo, was empowered by Cashman to radically overhaul the minor league chain. Big sums were spent on sports science and analytics and the psychosocial training of young players. One example among many: the Yankees hired a corps of high school instructors to teach language and life skills to recruits. From the bottom of their development system — the baseball academies in Latin America — to the Instructional and lower-tier minor league clubs, the Yankees invested heavily in cognitive and social development to boost their signees' chances to advance.

In countless ways that skirted the luxury tax, the team grew its operational base. "We were three people, total, in the New York office when I started in '01," says Afterman. "Now we're well over fifty here, and it's almost as many down in Tampa." That bifurcation of power — the Yankees are the only franchise in major league baseball with executive branches in two cities — was implemented by George in the '70s. Though he boasted the merits of internal "competition," his real motive seems to have been paranoia. "He thought he was King George" and worried that his courtiers "would get him" if he didn't spread them out, says a team insider. "He never really got that he actually *owned* the team and that no one could up and replace him."

The George years and their Medicean backstage jousts will be unpacked at bloody length in a later chapter. But the story of *this* team, the one that emerged from the last big fail in 2014, begins with Brian Cashman mending the gap between the northern and southern offices of the Yanks. All baseball decisions now run through him, though the team's three pillars — the heads of analytics, scouting, and business affairs — have a seat at his conference table. It isn't till they've had their say and reached consensus that Cashman brings a potential deal to Hal. Hal then talks to his own consigliere — his older brother Hank. "Hal knows the business, but it's Hank who knows baseball," says a staffer of the brother who stepped back in 2009 to look after the family's stables in Ocala. "He always kept a hand in after George died. Hal does nothing without going to him first."

Sometime before midnight on December 8, the Marlins came back to Cashman about the deal: they'd do the Stanton trade for a better hitter than Headley. Cashman quickly subbed in Starlin Castro, a moody star with a line-drive swing whose successor was ready and waiting: Gleyber Torres. All that remained was to make a second call, this one to Cashman's best player. "I phoned [Aaron] Judge to make sure I dotted every *i*," he says. "If there was an issue, I needed to vet it with him, not have him hear about it later from the *Post*."

It's rare that a GM consults his star before pulling the trigger on a trade; it's rarer still to consult a star who'd just finished his rookie season. But what a rookie season — and what a star. Judge was selfless and sweet-natured, a franchise talent with the character to match and shoulders that could carry a whole roster. His transformational power had goosed their stale lineup, made it feared and fun and must-watch TV, beginning with his batting-practice rockets. He carried that energy into the clubhouse, where the team adopted his spirit: free and easy, a group of kids thrown together, enjoying the ride of their lives. By the middle of May 2017, Judge was the face of the franchise; by July, he was the face of the sport. He was too nice a guy to be nettled by a trade, or too nice a guy to say so. But as Cashman had learned with the Jeter follies, a star's pride must be honored. Offering him early buy-in, or the illusion of it, can save a team's chemistry.

"Judge was like, 'Wow! That's incredible — what're you waiting for?!'" says Cashman. "I said, 'Well, it could affect your time in right.' He said,

'*Whatever*. I'll DH or play left!'" Through a variety of scouts, Cashman had heard the same thing about Stanton: he'd do anything the Yankees asked of him. Some of those sources were Marlins people; they so badly wanted out that "I knew I could trust their information," says Cashman. "It was, 'Here's what I got on Stanton . . . Now, can you hire me?!'"

Cashman sent the good news to Hal via text, knowing he'd gone to bed early. Then, having staged the heist of the year — adding the premium slugger in baseball to a monster lineup that had terrorized the league last season; clearing enough money to absorb Stanton's deal and still get under the luxury tax threshold; and giving back nothing but a couple of kids who were years from the major leagues — Cashman drained his beer and went straight to bed, leaving the fantasy fallout to the press. "I don't think like that," he says of the carnage to be wreaked by Judge and Stanton. "My job is to get as much talent as I can so we take a shot at the title. If I do my job well, we'll get multiple shots. The rest of it, the projections — who has *time*?"

Fifteen teams hold spring training in Florida; none of them host a venue as crass and sharp-elbowed as George M. Steinbrenner Field. You'd never mistake it for LECOM Park in Bradenton, an ancient facility where the Pirates play their games in front of a couple thousand seniors roused from naps, or Dunedin Stadium, the snowbird quarters for the Blue Jays that's essentially a high school diamond. No, "The George," as locals call it, is less a ballpark than a fortress, a monument to northern inhospitality on the fringes of sleepy Tampa. At the Stadium in the Bronx, you're accosted on the concourse by anti-terror troopers toting rifles. Here, a bulwark of permanently parked squad cars is posted at the gate, and ex-cops and prison guards work security after taking early retirement in New York. To the pinstriped tourists with their Crocs and canes, limping past the guards at the metal detector, the message of this place is, *We SEE ya, pal. Watch where you're pointin' that foam finger.*

For ten years, Joe Girardi looked and acted like one of those uniforms patting people down. It wasn't just the crew cut and bulging forearms, the severity of the pious Christian soldier. He managed games with such clenched-fist tightness, you feared he'd have a stroke making a mound trip. Even with four-run leads, he'd haunt the top step, the skin of his jaw stretched to its break point.

A bright, dexterous man who was rarely outmaneuvered and whose handling of his bullpen was superb, Girardi had the chops to become an institution, a skipper who stuck around for twenty years. But if he ever had a moment's pleasure managing the Yanks, you wouldn't have known it from his face. He was terse to the point of monkish with writers and came off badly on the postgame shows that he was contractually obliged to do. "We were shocked by that," said a Yankees executive who'd pulled for his hiring in '08. "He'd been great in the booth before taking over — sharp and relaxed, a good listen." Then he came in and "pissed off the writers by being the guy who gave 'em nothing." It was brutal to watch him in the media room, giving sour answers to softball questions while wearing a perma-frown. He never seemed to grasp that it was a privilege, even a thrill, to run the greatest franchise in American sports.

Each spring he would walk the clubhouse floor staring straight ahead, not so much as nodding at his players. As a manager explained to us several years back, there's a formula for working the locker room. "You spend ninety seconds a day checking in with each guy — just enough to let them know you care," he said. "Do less than that, they think you're a prick; do more, they think they run the show." Players, he went on, don't want a friend. What they want, without knowing it, is a dad. A Yankees executive picks up the point, saying there are three kinds of leaders. "There's the good dad, the stern dad, and the cool dad," he says. "We've had all three of them in a row now."

The good dad was Joe Torre, an avuncular skipper who steered with a light touch and a salty calm. With the exception of Joe Maddon, no manager in memory has had a feel for athletes' psyches like Padre Joe. Like the priest his parents hoped he'd become, he made everyone in the room feel seen and heard, especially guys struggling at the plate. Tino Martinez, who replaced the sainted Don Mattingly when he arrived via trade in '96, remembers getting off to a wretched start and being angrily booed that April. "Joe called me into his office one day — he'd made reservations at his favorite Italian restaurant for me. He said, 'Take your wife out and enjoy yourself. And by the way, you're my first baseman, end of story.'"

But the Torre who liked being loved by his players was reluctant to take them on. This was especially so with superstars: he refused to go after them when they dogged it in August or lost a step in the field. Near the end of Torre's tenure (he managed from 1996 through 2007), Cashman asked him to talk to Jeter about relinquishing the shortstop job. "Derek's defense was killing us, and I said to Joe, 'I look at him like a Robin Yount. He's awesome at fly balls, he'll be a great center fielder.' Joe said, 'Fine. I'll talk to him.'"

A couple of days later, Torre said that he'd spoken to Jeter and the shortstop had "no interest in doing that." Displeased, Cashman made a note to himself: he'd take it up with Jeter face-to-face. A year later, he and Jeter were having dinner at a restaurant on the Upper East Side. "I told him the reason Torre talked to you about moving to center was because of how bad you were defensively." Jeter was mortified: "'What're you talking about? You're saying my *defense* is bad?'" Torre, Cashman learned, had never talked to Jeter, nor did he ask Larry Bowa, his infield coach, to have the talk with him. "Bowa would come to me like, 'I'm working with him, Cash. We're trying everything we can!'" But he'd never mentioned defense to Jeter either — not at least according to Jeter. "One thing with Derek: he doesn't lie," says Cashman, who filed the matter away as a leadership lesson. "Now," he says, "I don't just *trust* people to do the job they're paid to do."

Sometimes the good dad's just the checked-out dad—the guy with his feet up on the coffee table while his teens stumble in at 3:00 a.m. For the last five seasons of his twelve-year stint, Torre let the clubhouse run itself. "He spent more time reading the *Racing Form* than going over scouting reports," says a club insider. He'd garnered four rings in his first five years, won the Eastern Division title ten times out of twelve, and managed the Yanks into October every season. Even when he fell short, Torre got rewarded: the addition of Jason Giambi after losing the '01 Series; the addition of Alex Rodríguez after dropping the '03 Series. The late-'90s team of twenty-something kids who'd matured and caught magic together was now an *Ocean's Eleven* cast of giant egos. The Gary Sheffields were rubbing shoulders with the Randy Johnsons and Mike Mussinas—twenty-five players, twenty-five publicists, as they say. Small wonder that, presiding over a squad of superheroes, Torre chose to rest on his laurels.

But it was the marketing of those laurels that undermined and eventually ruined his relationship with Steinbrenner. The breakup was years in the making, as the two had already begun drifting apart. Torre was 67, but popular enough to score one endorsement deal after another, as if he was still ten years younger and managing the golden-era teams of the late '90s. Steinbrenner never bought into Torre's celebrity, though: he seethed that these were *his* Yankees, not Joe's, and didn't appreciate being shoved off the stage. That, more than money or the championship drought, spelled the end of Torre's run in the Bronx.

In Girardi, Cashman chose the anti-Torre: an avid overpreparer who'd speak the truth to his stars and take advantage of the data set before him. Both men believed in the virtues of structure: you put together a plan and a staff to carry it out, then communicate it constantly up the line. Cashman, who'd won concessions when he re-upped in

2005 — the power to make decisions, to grow the New York office, and to bolster his major league scouting staff — had binders and spreadsheets on player matchups and now a manager eager to use them. Girardi showed up early to sit with his coaches, poring over heat maps and pitch progressions, the first wave of deep-dive analytics. What *wasn't* in those folders was the softer stuff: intel on his players as human beings. "He didn't listen to their music, didn't watch the movies they watched — he had no interest in what interested them," says an executive. Beginning in 2012, word came up from the clubhouse: the players didn't *like* this guy. "Ten years ago, if they didn't like the manager, they still busted their ass for him. Not anymore. These guys are millennials. Now it's, who the fuck are *you*?"

By the end of '17, it was clear Girardi was done: he hadn't just lost the room, he'd lost his drive. In July and August, when the club stopped hitting, it seemed to team officials that he'd packed it in. He retreated to his office and wouldn't come out, even to talk to his coaches. "It was like he wanted to be home with his kids," says an executive. "I thought he was done with managing altogether." And then, out of nowhere, the lineup caught fire and Girardi reengaged in September. He navigated the wild-card win over the Twins, the ALDS upset of the heavily favored Indians, and the thrilling comeback in the ALCS when, down 0–2, the Yankees swept at home and returned to Houston leading 3–2. They were brought up short by two brilliantly pitched games, but Girardi had the hunger again. His team had made the turn, gotten young and kinetic, and was positioned for a long, heady run. Yes, his deal had lapsed, but he had credit in the bank: the championship team of 2009 and ten winning seasons out of ten. Having frog-marched the club through its wilderness years — that post-'12 stretch when Jeter was in decline, A-Rod was in disgrace, and the Yankees' farm teams sent no help till Sánchez arrived in '16 — he'd earned himself the right, he thought, to opt back in and reap the rewards of the next five years.

The Yankees' season ended on Saturday, October 21, when they were meekly blanked by the Astros. The following Monday, Cashman called Girardi: *Come in one day this week and let's talk this out.* Girardi drove down to the Stadium that Tuesday, eager to share his plans for 2018. But Cashman cut him off at the knee. We've got young players and we need a leader who gets them, a messenger with a new message, he said. Girardi was gobsmacked. He could barely respond, sputtering about stability and foundation. He'd gone in expecting a long-term deal; half an hour later, he left in tears. The next day he rang Hal Steinbrenner on his cell and begged him to save his job. Hal was empathetic but firm with Joe: it's Brian's decision, and I stand by it.

A month and a half later, the Yankees hired Aaron Boone after a methodical, drip-dry search. The fourth of six candidates they invited to New York, he was the guy with the shortest résumé in the room. Since retiring as a player in 2009, Boone had knocked around the airwaves for several years before landing a seat on ESPN's *Sunday Night Baseball*. He hadn't coached, let alone managed, a team at any level, nor been known, like Carlos Beltrán, another finalist for the job, as a skipper-in-training while he played. But he was a third-generation pro baseball player who oozed the game's texture and tradecraft. Since boyhood, he'd been a close student of the sport: as a five-year-old running around the Phillies' clubhouse (his father, Bob Boone, caught for ten years there), he was famous for mimicking every hitter's stance and every manager's walk to the mound. Like his brother Bret, he grew up to be an All-Star, but Aaron would blow out a knee as he entered his prime, then have open-heart surgery at thirty-six.

His move to the booth wasn't a lateral step: it was where he discovered his calling. He had a gift for drawing out everyone he talked to, even when he wasn't saying much. Wherever the *Sunday Night* crew went for games, he spent the two-day lead-up gathering intel and gossip, filing it for use on air. By the time he sat down with the Yankees last fall, he knew as much about the league as their pro scouts did — and some interpersonal things that they didn't. "He'd seen which teams get along and what made their clubhouse click," says a club insider. One factor those lucky teams had in common: a manager who knew how to get across to the new breed coming up.

November 17 was an all-day grind for Boone. It began with a three-hour boardroom meeting, where he laid out his vision to Cashman and six officials, each of whom got a vote. Cashman was struck by how open Boone was, how adroitly he handled being challenged. The metrics guys grilled him about in-game adjustments, those data-driven calls in late or close spots. The development staff asked how he'd work with kids who hit the rookie wall. Each fractal of his worldview was poked and prodded during a second, break-out session after lunch. "It was the car wash of car washes," says Tim Naehring, the Yankees' vice president of operations.

Boone ran a gauntlet of sit-downs that day; none was more important than the one with Jason Zillo, the Yankees' media chief. Zillo is no mere herder of the press — he's the man who teaches players to talk like Yankees. Since his promotion to the position in 2007, Zillo has become Cashman's messaging partner, shaping perceptions of the brand. What Zillo wanted to hear was that he'd have an asset in Boone, a guy who was good in the room. "This is a really likable team, a mix of great kids and some older guys that get it," says Zillo. "That didn't happen by accident. It took tons of scouting and preparation, and we want the world to see what we've got here."

When the process ended and team officials ranked the entrants, Boone's name was first on every ballot. If there was one thing that put him over the top it was the bracing air of freshness he exuded. He was young in a way that would translate to players, a forty-something guy in a backpack and hoodie who, if need be, could deejay the clubhouse. (Side note: Boone is a one-man karaoke bar. On elevators and treadmills, he's *constantly* singing, crooning vinyl-era rock tunes to himself. It's an endearing trait to players, if not his coaches, who can hear "Eye of the Tiger" only so much.) You didn't have to tell Boone to spend time in the clubhouse — you couldn't stop him from doing it if you tried. Nor was it a strain on him to care for his players: Boone cares about everyone he meets. "Aaron was always the kid who befriended kids with no friends," says his father Bob in a long phoner. "He's the *likable* Boone, a born entertainer," says his brother Bret. Bret adds that Aaron's health scare — a valve malfunction pinching blood flow to his heart required a complex operation that so spooked Boone that on the eve of surgery he wrote farewell letters beforehand to his kids — made him a "better person and better dad."

Boone, in short, was a paradigm shift: a guy who lived and breathed next-gen baseball and could convey that to the players. A new pecking order had emerged in the game: at the top of the table were bleeding-edge teams like the Astros, Cubs, Red Sox, and Dodgers. Beneath them was essentially everyone else — the clubs sitting behind the curve. Five years earlier, Cashman saw this future coming and scrambled full speed to catch up. Now he had the tech and the talent assembled; it was either go big or go backwards. In choosing Aaron Boone, he was making two statements. First, these Yankees would *lead* the revolution, not just rally from behind. And second, this was officially Cashman's team now. In tone and direction and all the ways that mattered, it bore his palm-print on the chassis.

In baseball — that temple of Talmudic rules that no one ever bothers to jot down — a newly hired manager usually waits till spring to address his players at large. To the extent that he reaches out, it's a call to his

frontline stars, or nudging emails to the player or two who underperformed last season. Not Aaron Boone: in his first week on the job, he
texted every Yankee to say hello. They were short, upbeat squibs — *Su-
per-amped! Can't wait for Tampa!* — though his note to Gary Sánchez
ran deeper. Sánchez, the brilliant but moody slugger, was brutal behind
the plate in 2017. He posted league-worst stats in passed balls and errors and was out of synch with his starters, most notably Sonny Gray
and Masahiro Tanaka. Never the best receiver, he nose-dived badly in
the second half, after dialing back his pregame catching work. He especially hated doing the wild-pitch drill, in which he'd flop to his knees
and block hundreds of balls that his coach bounced in the dirt. At some
point, he announced that he was done with that annoyance; reluctantly,
Girardi let it pass. If the manager put his foot down, he risked losing the
kid's bat, so prone was his catcher to long sulks.

That decision backfired in a slew of passed balls and muffled com-
plaints from the starters. By August, Girardi had had it with Sánchez,
critiquing his defense to the press. What he said wasn't harsh, even
by baseball terms — "it needs to improve, bottom line" — but it was
enough to blindside Cashman; he decided then and there that Joe was
gone. "Cash hates that kind of stuff — it reminds him of the old days,"
says a team executive. The reference, of course, is to Steinbrenner *père*.
Big Stein chased the tabloids as hard as he did rings, feeding shills at the
dailies blind quotes and backstabs that wound up getting bannered in
ten-point type. For him, any attention was good attention, his daily required dose of vitamin Q. For Cashman, bad press had the bitter stench
of a team gone off the rails. It reeked of desperation and internal chaos.
He wasn't *about* to tolerate needless drama.

"I'd heard about that," Boone says of the Sánchez beef, but he gave
it no play in his text. Instead, he was looking ahead, "stressing the positive" with the catcher. "It's important that I had a connection to Gary.
That's what I was focusing on."

Connecting with people is what Boone does; he seems to have no gear but ENGAGE. From the first day pitchers and catchers reported, he showed up in the clubhouse and made the rounds. He talked to each of the players as they dressed, putting eyes and ears on everyone. The exchanges weren't profound — *Hey, how are you? Get a good night's rest?* — but you sensed the collective relief among the guys. Under Girardi, they had to be in uniform and on the field by 9:30. Boone pushed those start times back by an hour, letting the players sleep in if they liked. He gave his veterans semi-days off when the young guys bused to road games. They could show up at the park, get an hour of hitting in, then go home and hang with their family at the pool.

Boone's address to the team on the first day of full squads was less an invocation than a bro-hug. He told his players they were beyond a good team: they had the "stuff to be a powerhouse," in his words. His talk lasted two minutes and finished mild — no raised voice or pumped fists. The players were nonetheless amped. "I was thinking, *Wow, this is different: a positive take on what we have*," said Austin Romine, the backup catcher. "He spoke to our energy, our chemistry here. He's someone who's had big hits in big games and knew what it was like." David Robertson, the stellar reliever of ten years, put it in veteran terms. "It's just a younger vibe," he said with a shrug. Somewhere in the Bronx, Cashman was smiling.

Taken all around, Boone's spring training was a success — and for writers, a crashing bore. There were none of the usual tropes to milk for plot lines — no homegrown veterans approaching their walk year, no holdover feud between manager and mulish star. Nor were there signs that the players felt burdened by the great expectations for this group. Instead, what came across was something subtle but essential: *these guys really like each other*. It is hard to overstate how important that is, and how rarely you find it in sports. Most teams are chains of tiny island-states that do, or don't, align for seven months. The Latin guys hang and play cards in their corner, the white guys gossip in gaggles of three or four, while the black guys — a vanishing breed in the game — keep to themselves at their stalls. Other clubs divide along age or class lines, as happened with Yankee squads of the last decade: the stars in corner lockers with their coteries grouped around them, while the rest of the guys clump somewhere in the middle.

But this bunch was different — radically so. It began with the veterans, who made it their business to take some weight off of the newbies. CC Sabathia, the sage of eighteen years, brought many of the young arms under his wing and fed them every morning at his locker. Justus Sheffield, Chance Adams, Dillon Tate, Ben Heller — they all sat around him and spooned up what he taught, some of which didn't concern baseball. Three years removed from a dark night of the soul — the steep decline of his pitching prowess, the erosion of cartilage in both his knees, and a prolonged stint in rehab for alcohol addiction — Sabathia had become the guru of this team, a gregarious giant enjoying every second of his last days in the sun. He had recast himself as a precision pitcher, using movement and deception to get hitters out after a lifetime of power pitching. It was a stunning resurrection, and what came through him now was joy: a boom box of a laugh that bounced off walls and carried to the far side of the room.

Laughter was also what you heard from Didi Gregorius's locker; his stall should've been named The Comedy Store. Gregorius, the human emoji and chief tummler of the New York Yankees — he leads the team in dance steps, secret-society handshakes, and Gatorade buckets dumped on late-game heroes — is a running feed of jokes and online chirping. Every morning, he made a loud circuit of the room, spouting an Esperanto of infectious nonsense to anyone who would listen. This bunch of kids grew up together and developed a frisky bond; if there's a word that describes this team it's *coltish*. Though Didi wasn't one of them (he arrived via trade), the vibe they play with is his. His smile and his energy are gravitational — no one in the room escapes their pull. Smartly, the Yankees gave their phenom, Gleyber Torres, the locker next to Gregorius's. A sweet, eager kid with a tenuous grasp of English, Torres attached himself to Didi's side; the two of them would chat for hours in fluent Spanglish. (Didi, from Curaçao, speaks four languages and has invented a fifth for Twitter. It's largely indecipherable but runs heavy on fire signs and baby-bottle symbols.)

His silliness notwithstanding, Didi leads by achievement. Over the last couple of years, he's become a stealth assassin, a singles hitter who has learned to pull and use the lightning in his wrists. With a whipsaw swing that sprays liners to right and seems to square up every ball he strikes, he's emerged as the Yankee you least want to face in late-and-close situations. In what passed for the surprise of an otherwise sleepy spring, Didi forced Boone to move him up in the order. He left Tampa as the three-hole hitter, wedged between Judge and Stanton. On a team with thunder at every position and enough talent to endure the coming bumps, Didi had made himself a unicorn, the one man in the room they couldn't replace.

But the truest tell of a happy team is what it does postgame. Day after day, this group would stick around for a half-hour longer than needed, lingering in their stalls to kibitz and joke and make plans to meet for dinner. (Many nights they piled out to Ruth's Chris or Bern's, sharing pitchers and filets and just the *occasional* jaunt to Thee DollHouse.) The guy who stayed the latest — and was often first to the park — was Giancarlo Stanton. "G," as the players call him, could've phoned it in all spring. He was the reigning MVP and most lethal hitter in baseball; no one would have blinked if he'd coasted through March, then kicked it up a notch the last week down there. "G was here earlier than anyone else — that shows you how committed he is," said Judge. "He didn't have to prove anything to anyone; we all knew what a great hitter he was."

Stanton, for his part, was not convinced. "I'm *way* way off," he said, sheathed in sweat, after a three-hour session in the batting cage. Like all great hitters, he's obsessed with his hands and how they synch with his hips. The prior June, two months into the season, he'd drastically switched his stance. He'd moved his lead leg close to the plate and kicked his rear leg out; you could read the number on the back of his jersey as you toed the rubber. That severely closed stance is nearly extinct these days; hitters have opened up now to pull with power, not dump soft singles into right. Stanton, the contrarian, bucked the trend, pointing his left knee at the second baseman. That "kept my hips from leaking out and my bat in the zone longer," he said. Suddenly, it was impossible to keep him in the park. In the ninety-three games after he made the change, he clubbed forty-two homers and hit .284; twenty of those bombs went the opposite way. Still, it's a stroke that needs constant calibration. Stanton spent the month of March under the hood, taking hundreds of swings every morning.

Stylistically, he's mismatched with New York. Stanton is low key about his handlers, drives no sleek exotics, and has no strategic plan to grow his brand. He's a reclusive star who, given his druthers, would field questions once a month from a pool reporter. He spent eight years in Miami, where he addressed three writers in the clubhouse after games. But at the Yankees camp in Tampa, he was affronted by *fifty people* roaming the room for quotes; often there were ten or twelve lined up at his stall. His savior was Brett Gardner, the wise old head whom the Yankees lockered beside him. Calling the writers over, Gardy talked for ten minutes so Stanton could get dressed and gather his thoughts. It was the team's way of saying, *We got your back, G.*

On his half-days off, when the kids bused a couple of hours to play the Pirates or Blue Jays, Stanton hung back at the ballpark alone, grinding down and sanding his swing. The Yankees do indoor hitting in a tunnel beside the clubhouse — four batting cages that are open to the players any time of the day or night. The sound of a bat as it barrels up a ball is a jolt to the ears outdoors; *inside,* the effect is like hearing an M-80 blow every fifteen seconds.

BANG ... BANG ... BANG ... BANG ...

It was 11:00 a.m. when Stanton got in the cage. Eleven turned to noon, then 1:00 p.m.

BANG ... BANG ... BANG ... BANG ...

1:00 p.m. became 1:30.

"He almost done?" Woody, the lone guard, was asked.

"Not yet," Woody said.

1:45.

"Now?"

"Almost."

Finally, at 2:00 p.m., Stanton came from the tunnel. His shorts and logo T-shirt were soaked. Even at rest, his face says, *Back off,* and his brows naturally flare in a frown. If Da Vinci had drawn Ares, he'd look like Stanton. That bat of his could use planets for fungos.

He was displeased with the way his morning's swings had gone, and it didn't lift his mood to answer questions. "This is how I'm wired," he said of his session and the hell he'd unleashed for three hours. "There's so much failure in this game: you're supposed to fail seven out of ten." He paused to mop his brow with the heel of his shirt. The veins in his arms stood up and saluted. "I can't deal with that," Stanton said sharply. "I'm here to get my mind and body right."

And with that, he marched off and clattered down the concourse, to have a stern word with his mind and body.

2

DÉJÀ VU:
HAMMER TIME IN FENWAY

It's always loony in Toronto.

Fenway Park's a freak show of frat-boy berserkers seated too close to the grass. Citi Field's a bar brawl waiting to break out, Mets and Yanks fans mean-mugging each other the moment they park in Lot E. But the Rogers Centre in Toronto is a special slice of greasy: it's what happens when you mix industrial vats of Molson with Canadian dislike of crowd control.

The Yanks are used to fielding people's worst when they're on the road. It's the tax they pay on their power and privilege: getting jostled by stalkerazzi and eBay hounds in the lobby of their four-star lodging; hearing game-long airings of class resentments from the mutants on the third-base rail; and being heckled by people with all-purpose rage at anything New York–connected: *A-Rod Sucks!* . . . *Hillary for Prison!* . . . *Make America Gay Again!* The hating is so shameless that even a mensch like Aaron Judge occasionally takes the bait and fires back. Last summer, in US Cellular Field, he was showered with mama-jokes by a sociopath sitting in the right-field stands. (Judge, adopted by high school teachers, is fiercely protective of his parents.) He came up in the fifth and smoked a heat-seeking tracer in the vicinity of where the fan was screaming. As he rounded first base, Judge glared in his direction

and mouthed something under his breath. When asked what he'd muttered to/about the fan, Judge, the soul of prudence, demurred. "If it's all
right, guys, I'll keep that to myself."

Because the threat is real — and because they are the Yankees — the
team always travels with a force contingent: two burly ex-cops who
walk point for the players and an undercover detail to guard their flank.
It's a useful deterrent when they're going to the park, but once they
arrive, all bets are off. Then it's on their hosts to patrol the Yankees'
clubhouse, to protect their relievers in the right-field pen, and to keep
the hockey goons off the roof of their dugout. The Blue Jays fail badly at
all three tasks. There's a shocking dearth of Toronto cops in and around
the tunnel, and no — as in zero — ushers or guards manning the bullpen grounds. (This is especially vexing because the Rogers Centre still
sells beer in cans; it's the last stadium in major league baseball to arm
patrons with metal projectiles.) Worse, though, is the scene on the dugout roof. Drunkards crawl out there during batting practice, banging
the steel sheath with their fists and feet and screaming at the players
beneath them. If that happened in New York, they'd be handcuffed and
booked; in Toronto, vendors sell them more beer.

For these and other reasons, Toronto was the last place in baseball
the Yankees wanted to start their season. In the fourth week of March,
when the roof is closed and fans pack the party deck in center, it's pun-
ishingly loud and day-drunk hostile: no one wearing road grays feels
secure. Nor should they: for a decade, the Yanks have been bullied in
Toronto, playing sub-.400 ball there since 2010. What this 2018 group
needed, right from the jump, was a booster shot of fuck-you defiance: a
statement-making blast from one of the three bulls stacked in the middle of their order. In the top of the first, with one out and one on against
J. A. Happ, the Jays' starter, Giancarlo Stanton stepped in. He watched a
strike go by, then flicked his wrists at a pitch on the outer black.

The ball *vaporized* off his barrel, a phosphorescent pea to the first-deck seats in right-center. Traveling 117 miles per hour in a blue-light hurry before scattering fans in the fourth row, it was the hardest-hit homer to the opposite field since baseball started tracking these things. The rollicking crowd fell back as if gut-punched, giving a collective groan. Even Stanton's teammates lost their breath, grabbing the arm of the guy next to them in schoolboy glee as he calmly rounded third and headed home. When he crossed the plate and banged forearms with Sánchez, Stanton effectively told those forty-eight thousand people: *WE'LL be the bullies from now on, thanks.*

Happ, a cerebral lefty who had given the Yankees fits, collected himself and kept the Jays around. He was pitching cautiously into the fifth, dotting his four-seamer in and his two-seamer just off the plate, when Judge worked a walk with two outs. Up stepped Stanton in a 2–0 game. He fell behind in the count, then pummeled a slider, booming it off the wall on a bounce. Judge scored easily from first base; Stanton would come around on a Sánchez double. Happ was yanked, and the Jays were cooked; they never made a peep in a 6–1 loss. But Stanton had a closing statement. In the top of the ninth, facing Tyler Clippard, the ex-Yankee with a funky changeup, Stanton reached out and golfed a three-two hanger off the end of his bat. This time the Toronto outfielders barely budged, craning to watch his space-shot in flight. The homer carried 434 feet to center, landing in the Flight Deck boxes.

When Stanton got back to the dugout, his teammates ignored him, turning away and stanching their grins. "I was about to get up and give him a high-five, but everyone was like, *no, no, no!*" said Brandon Drury, the young third baseman whom Cashman had acquired in a trade with the Arizona Diamondbacks. Judge and Gardner, who'd ring-led the prank, hid by the bat rack, blank-faced. Stanton got the joke and high-fived air, a big, sweeping dap with ghost Yankees. Then everyone laughed, trading rump-smacks and pounds. It was baseball dumbshow for *Welcome home, brother: from this day forth, you're one of us.*

Nobody wins a pennant on opening day; by the end of week one, that first game's a blur. But here was a team declaring itself, telling the league about its makeup and mission as it left the gate. The message, as propounded by Stanton's stat line: *You can't pitch to us.* If the lineup didn't batter you, it would grind you up — force you, over and over, to make your pitch. Every hitter in the order was a deep-count worker, waiting for the slider without much tilt or a cutter leaking over the plate.

"There's gonna be lots of nights where they just beat the shit out of you, and there's nothing you can do about it," said a pro scout on hand to watch the series. "That lineup has power up and down. They can burn you at any time."

Cashman talks a lot to his staff in New York about the concept of *redundancy*. It isn't geek-speak for the flow of the season or the effect of a four-hour game on bloodshot viewers. It's in-house code for Cashman's vision: a roster of players whose skill sets repeat and, where needed, can replace each other. "When we won in the '90s, we weren't built around stars, so we didn't miss a beat when guys went down," says Jean Afterman. "That's Brian's way: build a circular lineup that just rolls over and over."

Judge mirrored Stanton. Didi echoed Greg Bird. Gardner and Aaron Hicks swapped leadoff. So, too, the bullpen, where there were three legitimate closers if Aroldis Chapman got hurt. Chad Green and Dave Robertson owned the seventh inning; Dellin Betances had the eighth. Or at least that's how it looked on paper in April. In the event of a tight series or one of those three-week stretches without a planned day off, the Yankees could keep trotting out power on top of power. To be sure, the rotation was iffy beyond Luis Severino, the opening day starter and winner. Masahiro Tanaka was Dr. Jekyll and Mr. Hyde, toggling long stretches of mastery with funks when his splitter didn't split. Sonny Gray had a wipeout curveball — and no idea where it was going. CC Sabathia was Andy Pettitte redux, owning the edges with a late-life cutter and a two-seamer that broke the opposite way. Alas, he had no cartilage in his landing knee and spent parts of every season on the DL. As for Jordan Montgomery, the marshmallow lefty who'd put up plausible numbers as a rookie, he hadn't shown anyone he could last six innings — which is about what you expect from a fifth starter.

But every powerhouse is a work in progress, prone to script revisions and late-night edits. Such was the case during an early April exchange with Cashman:

"You looking for another starter?"

Cashman: "*Yup.*"

"Someone who can beat Verlander? You've got one in Severino."

Cashman: "*Yup.* I'd like to have two."

"Got anyone in mind?"

"*Nope.* No one starts talking till after the amateur draft."

A promise was made to get back to him about starters in June. But first, there was a brand-new season to launch — and an overhang of winter that wouldn't budge. The first month's weather was like a Tough Mudder trial: cold and raw and wet underfoot, a damp that prunes the skin between your toes. Players took the field in hoodies and masks, as if dressed for a nor'easter — or biowar. "I was *freezing,*" said Stanton, who'd looked mummified in right during a twelve-inning loss to Baltimore in April. For the second time in a week, he'd worn the platinum sombrero, striking out five times in a game. After starting off hot in Toronto's room-temp dome, he'd come home to the Bronx and gone cryogenic. He flailed at sliders far off the plate, stared at strike three under his hands, and was booed by bridge-and-tunnel types who gave him the finger while wearing *mittens.* Those first several weeks, they seemed to blame him for everything: the Yankees' lumbering 8-9 start; the cluster of injuries that cost them four players; and the track-signal problems that made the ride from Canarsie feel like a four-hour game against the Red Sox.

But it wasn't the cold rain and boos that iced Stanton. As he confided in a pensive sit-down at his locker, he "just felt lost in general." He was lost in the field, where, after eight years in right, he'd been shunted to left. He was lost in the Bronx, where "I don't know what street I'm on, what I'm wearing [for the weather]," or even "what I'm eating anymore." It wasn't an excuse, just a statement of fact: he was a creature of strict habits. Even switching spring training from the Marlins' Jupiter, Florida, camp had rattled Stanton's cage; he spent the weeks in Tampa groping for clues. "Look at my spring numbers — I shit the bed there too. I needed to settle in *wherever* I was."

Oddly, he had chosen to time-share his transition, splitting an apartment in Manhattan with A. J. Ramos, the ex-Marlins pitcher who'd become a Met over the previous summer. Any slack that might have bought Stanton went right out the window. The truck with his furniture got lost in transit and was weeks late arriving in New York. Between his sense of dislocation and the bitter Northeast spring, Stanton's swing went missing in April.

For beat writers hoping to get a sense of a new Yankee, the rules of engagement have changed. Twenty years ago, players sat at their lockers chatting, or they bantered in groups playing spades or poker at a card table off to the side. Nowadays, *no one's* at their lockers before games: they're in the trainer's room or the players' lounge or taking extra swings in the cage. If you buttonhole a guy en route to the tunnel, you feel the stares of thirty writers on your neck: *Hey, give someone else a shot, man.* It's been a catastrophe for beat writers and the people who read them, but neither party started this war.

Instead, put the blame in the lap of talk radio, which hijacked the conversation about the game. In the mid- to late '90s, when sports-chat took off as a fast-and-dirty earner for AM stations, ballplayers dialed in on their drive to the park and heard themselves flamed by Bruce from Wantagh. The shows were loops of spit-flecked self-pity as shut-ins, celibates, and six-pack soliloquists pinned their unhappiness to, say, the tail of Carlos Beltrán, whose ninth-inning whiff with the bases loaded in '06 cost callers their sacred birthright: a Mets World Series. (Poor Carlos, frozen in amber by that Adam Wainwright hammer. Never mind that he was the reason the Mets *made* it to the playoffs, posting heroic numbers all season.)

These callers were egged on by their hosts: hot-take hucksters and CPAP breathers who often knew as little about the game as their listeners. Their job wasn't to reflect and inform; it was to stir the pot. Any mistake a player made, or any quote he gave that smacked of *me* not *we,* would be picked to death on-air from noon to night. And so, sensibly, New York athletes learned to zip it. What they gave the writers now were decoupaged koans about "playing for each other" and taking it "one game at a time" while being "on the same page" "at the end of the day." Nor was it only the players who were piping down now. Managers who'd always talked to writers before games suddenly shut the door to their office. Now they only spoke when required, doing pre- and post-game briefings in the pressroom. Some version of this has happened in every sport, but baseball is the game that's been most impacted. Thirty years ago, it was like a brokered romance between the players and fans. The players played the game, then talked about it after, giving their candid takes to the writers. The fans watched the game and read the dailies over coffee, then kibitzed over details at work. They didn't *really* know the players, but had a sense of them regardless, and that was good enough to grow affections. Now, thanks to Twitter, there's less distance between the sides, but a mutual antipathy fills the space.

Once in a while, however, you get lucky with a player — and if you press your luck, gold falls out of his mouth. Stanton is such a player: he normally has an armored bearing, but if you ask the right question at just the right time, his visor flips up for twenty minutes. After one of the five rainouts he weathered in the early going, he was cornered at his locker after a shower. He'd already addressed the media about his poor start in New York and, to his credit, answered every query. But no one had thought to ask him about the near-death experience of being struck in the face with a fastball. That question was put to him after the other writers left. Stanton flinched — then spoke for a solid half-hour.

In September 2014, during a game in Milwaukee, Stanton took a heater flush in the face from the Brewers' starting pitcher, Mike Fiers. When a strong-armed thrower releases a pitch, a major league batter has less than half a second to react to the ball in transit. Honest hitters talk about a vanishing point: that spot in a ball's flight, about eight feet out, where they suddenly lose sight of it. It isn't that they blink — the pitch literally *disappears* in those last milliseconds of travel. A good hitter's swing path, framed by instinct and training, is still just guesswork on his part. So is his decision to duck a beanball. When he sees it leave the hand and bend toward his head, the batter must start his bailout well before arrival — and even *that's* a guess about where the ball is going.

Stanton was leading the league in homers that year, and the Brewers were buzzing him up and in, trying to move him off the plate. Fiers's 0-1 two-seamer was a waste pitch inside — but it just kept biting and rising. Stanton didn't budge as the pitch bore in; he lost sight of it near the plate. "From here to that couch — I never saw it after that," he said, pointing to a sofa in the Yankees' clubhouse. "All I felt was impact, and then falling on the ground. The whole side of my face was gone — I felt sharp pieces in my mouth. I was trying to be soft with them because I didn't want to choke, but the pain was excruciating."

The fans at Miller Park fell silent. Trainers raced to the plate. They tried to roll Stanton onto his back, but he fought them, unable to speak. His mouth had filled with blood, and, in panic, he thought he'd drown if he didn't stay down on his side. "I was afraid I'd swallow my teeth," he said, patting the side of his face where a hole had been lanced by the impact of the ball. At the hospital, a doctor "put his finger right through it, like I was a fish he'd hooked." Multiple bones were broken; shards of teeth lodged in his lips. That autumn, he underwent a string of operations to fuse the breaks in his lower jaw and cheekbone. When the swelling subsided, teeth were implanted, but there was nothing to be done for the nerves. A swath of his left cheek is permanently numb. "I can't feel that," he said, tracing a two-inch crescent from his lip to his cheek. "I've gotten used to it — sort of. But when I smile, that part won't go up as high."

Stanton spent most of that winter healing — but the hard work was psychic, not physical. He now had to train his mind to wall off fear: his livelihood depended upon it. "I knew if I was scared, my career was over — I might as well find something else to do." He wouldn't say *how* he'd willed himself not to flinch; hitters who've been beaned and seriously injured are loath to deep-dive that process. All of them have heard of the tragedy of Tony Conigliaro. A generational talent and supernal slugger who'd hit a hundred home runs for the Boston Red Sox before he turned twenty-three, Tony C., as he was adoringly known at Fenway, took a Jack Hamilton fastball an inch below his eye in the summer of '67. Rico Petrocelli, who was in the on-deck circle, described the sound of a face collapsing as a "squish . . . like a melon hitting the ground." Conigliaro survived his crushed cheekbone and jaw, but the damage to his career was catastrophic. He returned a year and a half later, battling fear and blinkered vision to earn Comeback Player of the Year. The damage to the retina was progressive, however, and he was forced out of baseball by thirty. Seven years later, he suffered a massive stroke. Conigliaro lay in a vegetative state till his merciful death at forty-five.

Stanton, who has never watched a clip of his own beaning, didn't need reminders of that day. But he got them, nonetheless: during his first months back, he was tested by pitchers *trying* to throw inside. "It happened every game in my first at-bat — and yes, that made me mad," he said. "If you go that far in, then you're doing it on purpose. And if you miss your spot and hit me, then *that* was on purpose too." To protect himself, he added the C-flap extension that bolts to the side of the helmet. Still, it didn't cover his amygdala, the lizard part of the brain that screams *DUCK!* Stanton somehow managed to mute that voice, standing up to his brushback hazers.

Marcus Thames, the Yankees' hitting coach, was asked what he'd said to Stanton during his early-season slump. Thames gave a laugh and shrugged. "*Nothing*," he said. "The man knows his own swing. There's nothing I could tell him he doesn't know."

That take on Stanton tallied with what we saw: he has a dead-sure grasp of who he is. He was impeccably raised by mixed-race parents who opened the world to him. His father Mike and mother Jacinta were postal workers in the San Fernando Valley. They traveled ambitiously on vacation — to China and India and Africa — and anointed him at birth with names befitting an explorer: Giancarlo Cruz Michael. He went by "Mike" as a kid to honor his dad and was so known when he was drafted by the Marlins. But like his parents, he was stricken with the travel bug and spent his winters trekking Europe and the Middle East. In late 2011, he came back from Italy and decided to honor his birthright. From then on, he would be known as Giancarlo Stanton, and tough nails to any fans who found that boujee. As he told the *New York Times* at the time, he didn't care what people thought: "You got something unique, you don't run from it. You embrace it."

Big leads being squandered by their middle relievers, head-scratching slumps for half their vaunted lineup (at one point or another Stanton, Sánchez, Gardner, and Neil Walker were all hitting below .200), and a string of sloppy starts from Tanaka and Gray — the Yankees played, for much of the month of April, like a team seeking shelter and strong drink. They'd just dropped three of four to the awful Orioles when they flew up to Boston in a funk. It was 37 degrees as they took the field for the annual recommencement of hostilities. As Yankees past and present will freely tell you, there's nothing like setting foot in Fenway Park to shake your faith in human progress. The seats are so close that you hear every *fuckyourmothah* from the Cask 'n Flagon regulars in row C. "It's the one place where, right after the Anthem, you want to get back in the dugout," a retired star told us before the game. "They're F-bombing you with 'A-Rod this' and 'Jee-tah that!' even before the song dies out."

Not that there's any refuge in the dugout. It's the smallest one in baseball, a pea-green foxhole at just a thin roof's remove from the jolly stompers. Ditto the bullpen, where, in 2003, a *security guard* threw punches at Yankee players. That old joke about hockey gets echoed at Fenway: it's a fight where a ball game breaks out. Thurman Munson versus Carlton Fisk. Bill Lee versus Graig Nettles. A-Rod versus Varitek for the heavyweight belt. And now here was a Yanks team run by Aaron *FUCKING* Boone, the same guy who, in '03, crushed the spirit of New England with his series-ending bomb in the ALCS. True, each club had retooled its core ethos, building around princes like Judge and Mookie Betts, the best-behaved stars of their generation. And also true, all the heels were gone: without Papi and Pedro, Jeter and A-Rod, there were no goats on which to hang the horns.

But for the first time in ages, both teams had peaked at once, posting hundred-win talent that was coming of age and would battle, chest to chest, for half a decade. Both had surplus power, striking arms-race deals to bring in big-time boppers over the winter. (*We'll see your Stanton and raise you J. D. Martinez . . .*) And both teams had an ace, a shutdown closer, and sufficient stock to trade for a difference-maker. In the run-up to this series, there was more than a casual sense that the hate was hotting up again.

Game 1 was a wipeout: the Sox raked Severino, and the Yankees gave their hosts six unearned runs. (This was something of a theme to start the season. The Yanks made twelve errors the first two weeks, as if, in their haste to bludgeon opponents, they forgot to pack their gloves.) Game 2 began as another dud. New York bolted to an 8–1 lead, Tanaka seemed to rediscover his splitter, and then, because these teams are incapable of prolonged dullness, the game went to hell in a handcart. Early on, Tyler Austin had nicked Brock Holt with a hard but legal slide at second. Both teams left their dugouts in a show of . . . well, something: there was a lot of milling around and mean-mugging. But gas had been poured in a park that's pure accelerant, and in the seventh inning the bonfire erupted.

Joe Kelly, a bespectacled, hard-throwing reliever who's built like a kitchen match, tried *twice* to drill Austin with high heat. The second time he nailed him in the ribs. Austin slammed his bat down and went for Kelly, who ducked and threw a punch as bodies swarmed them. A lucky thing for Kelly: Austin is country strong, the country in question being *Bulgaria*. He's shorter than Judge and Stanton but thicker than both combined, with a trunk and neck framed of poured cement. "He could shred *anyone*," Judge said after the game, still burning off adrenaline from the brawl. If Austin had connected, said a second Yankee, "Kelly would've been in the hospital now."

Instead, Kelly found himself pinned against his dugout, with the rest of his overmatched squad. Entirely on their own, Judge and Stanton moved the pile, pushing the Red Sox roster up the first-base line in the most lopsided shoving match since Andy Kaufman. Backing up Judge and Stanton was Betances (six-foot-eight) and Sabathia (six-six); Sox combatants couldn't clear out fast enough. "I'm not trying to get involved with *any* of those guys, not just Stanton and Judge," said Holt, the second baseman who'd squawked at Austin. "They've got a pretty big team over there."

In the scrum, Judge had Kelly in a fierce half nelson and walked him from the mound as you would a child. He appeared to be keeping the peace, but was boiling mad, angrier than New York had ever seen him. "I *wish* someone had thrown a punch at me," he said. "That would've given me an excuse." Asked if he'd ever charged the mound himself, he said, "Not as a professional player." How about high school, or travel ball? "Sure," he said, curling a faint grin (or snarl). "There's always someone who wants to take a run at the big guy."

The Yankees were a sub-.500 team as the brawl game began on April 11, and the Sox were off to their best start ever. A week later, they'd sit at 17-2 and hold a seven-and-a-half-game lead in the division. But baiting their rival was an unforced error that they'd quickly come to regret. The fight catalyzed the Yanks, got their temper up, banded them together for the battle. They should have sent the Sox a thank-you note.

After flying to Detroit in a soaking rain that scrubbed most of a weekend series, the Yanks came home to their welcome wagon — better known as the Minnesota Twins. For years, the fat-cat Yanks have treated the Twins like undocumented labor living below-stairs. They typically outspend them two-to-one for talent, out-earn them three-to-one in regional TV money, and outdraw them by more than a million fans a year. True, the Twins are stable and smartly run, but the rules of sports capitalism still apply: big bank takes little bank over time.

The Yankees have thrashed the Twins in the regular season (owning them 82–31 since 2002) and used them as their stepladder in the postseason, ousting them straight five times to advance. In the wild-card game that launched their run in '17, the Yanks spotted the Twins three runs in the first, then snatched them right back in the bottom of the frame with a heartbreaker three-run homer. The man who golfed that homer — and may have saved the Yanks' season — was their all-of-a-sudden slugger, Didi Gregorius.

While New York fans were mooning over Sánchez and Judge and

projecting the second coming of a Core Four cadre, Gregorius was quietly staking his claim as the indispensable Yankee. Set aside his value in the clubhouse a moment and consider his artistry in the field. He plays the best shortstop the Yankees have seen since Jeter in his mid- to late twenties. Didi eats up dribblers with a glide-step shuffle, spins in the hole to fire darts across his body, and vacuums bad hops with a matador's flourish. Everything he does is baseball ballet, an airborne expression of joy. Even his swing is a thing to behold: that buggy-whip snap of the barrel through the zone and the *crack* of the ball off his bat. In April, he kept the Yanks afloat with key hits when they slumped for several weeks; posted career bests in every offensive stat that mattered; and slugged his way into the cleanup spot, slotting between Judge and Sánchez. In a year of grand theater and smash debuts, Didi pulled the biggest coup of all: he made everyone forget about Saint Derek.

He was no one's savior when he got to New York in an unremarked trade in 2015. With the Diamondbacks, Gregorius was a reckless chaser who didn't hit lefties or drive the ball. He had the fast-twitch speed to steal bases and pressure pitchers but couldn't get on enough to scare them. It was impossible to walk him, even if you tried: his base-on-balls rate ranked 219th out of 232 hitters with 1,000 at-bats. Forty percent of his swings were at balls outside the zone, which also ranked him 219th. "It's not easy for me to lay off pitches," he explained. "Even in the cage, I swing at everything because I know I can get my barrel on it." To be sure, Gregorius was a glove guy growing into his power when Cashman swung the deal for him. If he ultimately topped out as a .260 hitter who, on occasion, reached the short seats in right, the Yankees would have settled for that. But Mike Fishman, the Yankees' data analysis chief, saw more in Didi's aerodynamic frame.

Unlike Judge and Stanton, most baseball players are smaller now than they appear on camera. If you spend any time in the Yankees' locker room, you're distinctly underwhelmed by what you see. Sánchez, who reads as thickly muscled in pinstripes, is packing a soft paunch under his shirt; his chest and thighs are thick but undefined. So, too, Severino, who's barely six feet and whose shirtless trunk will never make *Men's Fitness*. Didi, on the other hand, is bigger and more pneumatic than you might suppose from your couch. At six-foot-three, he has a sprinter's body: broad and coiled through the delts and quads, with long-strand muscle below the waist that's quick to fire at a pitch. There's power in that setup, but it hadn't been unlocked: he'd hit thirteen homers, *total*, his first three years. What held Didi back was his intransigence: he refused to take instruction from his failures.

Enter Fishman, a tall, recessive chap with the pallor of a basement sabermetrician. Though he speaks in a voice you have to strain to hear as you sit in his windowless office, his input rings as loud as any executive's in the building. Indeed, these cloud-based Yankees are the creatures of Fishman's metrics. He and his staff of fifteen — the biggest in the game — have built a data platform that spans the sport, covering every level from high school up. When Cashman hired him in 2005 at the suggestion of Billy Beane, Fishman founded the Yankees' Analytics Department as a systems-ops staff of one. He was a midtwenties stathead with a math degree from Yale and a passion for baseball's fourth dimension, numbers.

Growing up a Mets fan in Greenwich, Connecticut, Fishman had been one of those boys who saw the game as a science, learnable less through instinct than charted proofs. He and his friends spent entire weekends in Strat-O-Matic orgies; even then, before the advent of fantasy quantization, he penned handwritten reports on every player in baseball, tracking their swing rates and hot zones.

Out of college, he took a job at an insurance company but never stopped pining for the game. Then, in '03, Fishman read *Moneyball* and saw his future flash before his eyes. "I'd spent my whole life applying math and stats to baseball, but didn't think I could make a career of it."

He threw himself into a pair of research projects and sent the findings to thirty major league teams. At the '04 Winter Meetings, he was one of those pale lemmings hoping to land a sit-down with a club. Beane was the only GM who talked to him. He peppered the kid with questions about his research, but ultimately hired someone else for the position. (Fun fact: the aspirant who won out, Farhan Zaidi, general-managed the LA Dodgers and was subsequently hired by the SF Giants.) Still, the interview gave Fishman hope. A year later, he landed an audience with Cashman, who hired him a week after their meeting.

Fishman, thirty-nine now, heads an exhaustive staff that functions as the Deep State of the Yankees. They've built an interface that can be accessed by anyone with the proper clearance. That includes the quants down the hall in their conference room (where a larger-than-life Darth Vader prop accosts you at the door), the baseball-ops guys in the Tampa office, the analysts embedded with each minor league team in the Yankees' system, and their pro and amateur scouts around the world. On that global platform are stat-packs and video of *every single player in organized ball anywhere,* be it the backup catcher of the San Diego Padres or a high school sophomore reliever in Los Altos. "If you're playing baseball somewhere, you're in our system," says Fishman, whose desk is as crowded as a commodity trader's. There are four flat-panels nesting before him, though he's careful to snap them off when hosting visitors. What isn't in view are a sprawl of reports and color-coded spray charts of Yankee hitters. Paper has gone the way of ten-year deals these days; the front office speaks to its players via screens now.

In the spring, each Yankees player is assigned an iPad Pro and then emailed daily updates to browse. Everything is on there: his lifetime at-bats against the day's starter; pitch-over-pitch analysis of how that team attacks him; heat-maps reminding him where and what to swing at; and trend-line reviews of how he's doing. Five years ago, players bristled at these pokes: how dare some geek who'd never played the game tell them how to break a four-day slump? But baseball has become a millennial's sport, and millennials live entirely through their screens. When they aren't on the field, players are on their phones and tablets, streaming Netflix or Fortnite or Statcast footage instead of living large at the clubs.

From the day Didi arrived, Fishman pounded the obvious home: stop chasing hard stuff up and away — all you do is hand the pitcher a gift. And Didi got it, to a point: he cut back on his strikeouts and began to drive the ball with regularity. Each year his slugging percentage pushed up starkly. In '17, when he lost a month to a shoulder strain and *still* hit twenty-seven homers, he trailed only Judge and Sánchez in power production. But Fishman mined the numbers at season's end and spotted something subtle that alarmed him. Pitchers threw him "fewer balls in the zone," said Fishman, hoping that Didi would grow impatient and help them out.

And so, in the spring of '18, Fishman sent one of his staffers to *show* Didi what was coming. Zac Fieroh, an analyst, played clip after clip of pitchers who teased him away. The session was Didi's *aha* moment: he vowed then and there to buy in fully. Asked later to elaborate on that promise, Didi declined to go deeper. For a man as relaxed as he is around players, he's decidedly less at ease with the press. He's mastered the team's *tao* of ten-word answers: a complete thought reduced to a single sentence, then a nod that ends it, full stop.

"The game is about numbers, one way or the other," he said in April.

Hoping for more of that thesis, the questioner prodded. *Yes?*

"Even if you say you're not about that, you are."

So you were receptive to what the analyst showed you that day?

"I was open to what he said. I kind of knew it already."

This was Didi-speak for, *Are we done yet?* His emphatic nod said, *Yes, in fact, we are.* Nor was there any luck to be had pulling details out of Fishman. But whatever Fieroh said to Gregorius in March, it clearly hit home with him. From the day he flew north to start the season, Didi was a different player. For a solid month, he led the Yankees in everything — batting average, homers, RBIs, and OPS. Actually, he led the *world* in most of those things: he was the runaway Player of the Month in the American League. When everyone but Judge was stymied at the plate, Didi put the team on his shoulders.

The heavy lifting started in the home opener against Tampa: Didi had two homers, eight ribbies, and three runs scored. From that point, the hits just kept on coming. Over the first five weeks, he batted .476 on pitches to the inner half and smashed nine of those mistakes for homers. He was barreling more pitches than he had in the past: per Statcast, his ratio of hard-hit balls was the best of his career. Another gauge of his growth was pitch selection. He had as many walks as strikeouts for the month, and that prudence paid off in productive outs. His two sac flies in the brawl game against the Sox were one less than he totaled his first two seasons.

But for all of Didi's heroics, the Yanks were treading water when the Twins came to town in late April. In the first game, a 14–1, clear-the-pipes blowout, Didi capped the attack with a grand slam. He had another bomb the next night in an 8–3 laugher, and a third one in game 3, a 7–4 stroll. In the four-game massacre that jumped the Yankees' season and sent them on a torrid three-week roll, Didi was the life of the party. He homered in four straight games to kick-start the spree, drove in thirteen runs over a seven-game stretch, and practically outscored opponents by himself, coming across nine times in those games.

At last, the club was having fun and bashing people's brains in. They scored sixty-four runs in a nine-game win streak, tapped the brakes in a 2–1 loss to Houston, then ripped off eight wins in a row. Over that three-week stint, they won seventeen of eighteen and beat the best in the West in their own parks — a three-game sweep of the Angels in Anaheim and three-of-four revenge wins in Houston.

There's a reason they put a roof on the former Enron Field when they opened it in the spring of 2000: without one, you'd baste in your own bacon fat as you watch a game in July. For anyone not raised in a convection oven, the heat in Houston is unendurable after Memorial Day. Even April is a bad-hair month; you can wait all day for a breeze that never comes. But when they close the accordion roof, you trade heat stroke for tinnitus. The place is as loud as a jet propulsion lab.

Years ago, when the Twins played their games in the Metrodome, someone metered the noise there during the playoffs. It reached 125 decibels, or about 40 more than needed to do lasting damage to your ears. It wasn't *quite* that raucous when the Yankees returned to Houston to close the ALCS in October 2017, but the din was so piercing — and so persistent for nine innings — that it clearly unnerved their hitters. In games 3, 4, and 5, all wins in the Bronx, the Yankees scored nineteen runs. They scored a total of *one* in games 6 and 7 — and three in the four games won by Houston there.

It was bloody loud again on April 30, when the Yankees pulled in for the series opener. Unlike Boston, where the abuse feels *personal*, here it's polyvalent, like the heat. The screaming is relentless, but there are assaults on other senses as well: the faint scent of cigarettes from the mezzanine level, where good old boys in Biggio jerseys watch on big TVs (Minute Maid Park is one of the last venues in sports to let fans smoke near the seating area); the sea of orange shirts distracting the batter's eye; and the grease-pit plume of charred meat grilling on the concourse ringing the field. (The place is as much a ribs shack as it is a ballpark. They serve barbecue in the press box. To the *bloggers*.) Picture yourself at a football game between SEC blood rivals: a huge crowd tanked on tailgate beers and a truckload of rebel spirit. Now dome that field in and brush hot sauce on it: that's what facing the Astros is like when you're playing them in their yard.

Games 1 and 2 of the four-game set were a rehash of October: the Yankees couldn't sniff Houston's starters. Charlie Morton cut them down as he did in the pennant clincher, K'ing ten in seven and two-thirds innings and sawing through the heart of the Yankees' lineup. He, like Justin Verlander, who stoned them in game 2, is a reclamation project worth saluting: the kind of big-armed pitcher on the wrong side of thirty that the Astros have made a specialty of reviving. Morton had labored for three teams over nine blah seasons, lost chunks of three years to hip and shoulder woes, and never won more than ten games. Other teams mistook him for a busted valise: he made four starts for the Philadelphia Phillies before a hamstring cost him the rest of 2016.

But Houston's analytics people saw something in Morton and made him a modest offer. Five years recovered from Tommy John surgery, he threw harder at thirty-three than he did at twenty-eight, and he had a great natural sink on his two-seam fastball. They tweaked his delivery to reduce the stress on his hips and showed him how to back-door hitters with his slider to either side of the plate. Suddenly, he was dotting his fastball where he wanted — and throwing it 98, with heavy spin. So too his sinker, which bored in at 95 and was impossible to hit when he was on. It was filthy that night in April: of the twenty-seven outs the Yanks made, twenty-two were by strikeout or grounder.

After the 2–1 loss, their clubhouse was silent; you could almost hear the click of throats tighten. As command pitchers do, Morton had exposed a weakness: the Yankees were clearly a hit-or-miss machine. They were patient, yes; they led the world in walks and had the highest on-base average in the league. But their run producers whiffed at an ungodly rate — once in three at-bats for Judge and Stanton, and one in four for Sánchez. That cost them, often dearly, in close games. Putting the ball in play lets you move along your runners and score manufac-tured runs when you need them. The Core Four Yankees were masters of the craft called "situational hitting." They'd get a guy aboard, mix a bunt with a stolen base, and bring him home with a routine fly to cen-ter. A man on third with less than two out? Getting him home is classic situational hitting. But it's become a lost art in this age of launch angles, and more's the pity too. It's a crucial tool to have when you're locked in a pitchers' duel — and it's make-or-break important in the playoffs.

That raised a second worry about these bulked-up Yankees: Were they built to storm the regular season but not to beat great pitching in the playoffs? What good would it do them to win a hundred or more games while breaking the season record for home runs if they tapped out in the divisional round? Their power and patience were limited virtues when it came to October. You can't wait out the starter then: he's only asked to go five innings. The last four innings are bullpen wars, a trick invented by the Kansas City Royals to win a title in 2015. Small matter that the Yankees have the deepest pen in baseball: at *some* point, you have to hand those guys a lead. And how, when your lineup whiffs fourteen times, are you supposed to jump in front of the Houston Astros?

The following night, the Yankees struck out *fifteen* times and lost their starting pitcher early on. (Jordan Montgomery left with elbow tightness; he'd end up needing Tommy John surgery and would be lost for the year.) Fourteen of those punch-outs were against Verlander, who'd returned to peak form at thirty-five. For most of his thirties, the former Cy Young winner seemed to be losing an argument with his body. He'd thrown more pitches than anyone in baseball since his rookie year (2006), and the wear and tear of those 2,400 innings told on his soft tissue. He had core muscle surgery in 2014, then missed a chunk of 2015 with a triceps strain. His fastball velocity dipped to the low 90s; hitters ignored it and ambushed his slider. He got some arm strength back in 2016 and was once again a good, if not great, starter. Then the Astros acquired him in the summer of '17 and performed their data magic.

They showed him high-speed film of a slider leaving his hand and pointed out that if he altered the angle at which he released it, he'd get a bigger sweep to left-hand hitters. The Astros also changed the grip on his bread-and-butter pitch: a high-spin fastball that stayed up. Suddenly, Verlander was untouchable — no one could get on top of his four-seamer. Everything he threw now was a strike until it wasn't; his K-to-walk ratio *tripled*. He was throwing as hard as he ever had, dialing up 100 in *late* innings. He could have been a Yankee, but his salary of $28 million had scared off Cashman and his staff. (Instead, they dealt for Sonny Gray, who earns a quarter of Verlander's money — and pitches like it.) That frugality cost the Yankees in the ALCS of '17. Verlander beat them twice, won series MVP, and was exactly the kind of star Big Stein would have leapt at: a knock-you-down ace who was as tough as East Texas. Somewhere, the old man was surely spinning.

But in the regular season at least, you can *outlast* Verlander. The Yankees forced him to throw 105 pitches, then jumped the Astros' closer, Ken Giles. They scored four runs off him to break a scoreless tie — and dispelled the building's hex on their bats. The next night, they beat their arch-nemesis, Dallas Keuchel; Stanton scorched him for a pair of homers and drove in the game's four runs. Playing loosey-goosey in the series finale, they got out to a fast lead, fell behind in the seventh, then broke the Astros' backs with a three-run ninth. It was a breathless end to a crackerjack month — and a glimpse of the wonders to come. Their big three hitters went oh-for-the-day, but the kids did all the damage at the end. Gleyber Torres drove in two in the ninth, and Miggy Andújar had two hits and the tying run.

Didi had carried this team as far as he could haul it; it was time for someone else to take the weight. It wouldn't be Judge, who was hitting homers but couldn't get a hot streak going. It wouldn't be Stanton, who raised his average thirty points but still looked lost at the plate. And it surely wasn't Sánchez, the sour enigma languishing at .200. No, the heroes were the kids at the bottom of the order: Torres, who'd lead the team in homers in May and win the Rookie of the Month Award at twenty-one, and Andújar, a doubles-hitting machine of twenty-three who always seemed to be standing on second base. Though neither player started the season in the bigs, they'd become the steadiest hitters on the sport's most potent offense. They earned about a million bucks, total, between them and showed up their betters by doing the simplest act in baseball: putting bat solidly to ball. Watching them do the small stuff — shortening their stride with two strikes, laying off splitters in the dirt — you wondered when the big guys would get the message: swing-and-miss icons don't win titles.

After their last game in Houston, the Yankees' clubhouse was Latin Quarter loud. Judge is the deejay, home and away: his iPhone starts the party when the Yankees win. (Rule number one in their locker room: No tunes after losses. *Ever.*) His playlist starts with Drake, but jumps to reggaeton: Bad Bunny, Nicky Jam, and — of course — Daddy Yankee. Ozuna was blasting over the PA system, and Severino, who'd thrown a shutout the night before, was shimmying at his locker to "Criminal." On a very young team with a *bachata* beat, everyone seemed to know the words. Aaron Boone was making the rounds, giving hugs and daps. Finding Andújar, he thumped him on the chest. "*Great* read!" he exclaimed of Miggy's decision to score from second on a shallow single. "That's what I'm talking about!" Andújar beamed like a travel-ball kid as Boone moved on to the next locker.

3

THE LITTLE GENIUS

Reporters who've gotten to know him learn that Brian Cashman has two modes of speech. The first, in front of cameras or with the pre-game press, is intentionally void of content. If it isn't the dead-fish-gray prose that writers used to get from Jeter, it's about an hour from going stale at the gills. Gazing at the mike, Cashman will arbitrage your question, hedging both sides to come out clean. Close Cashman readers can occasionally catch flecks of gold, but nothing you'd really take to the bank. He doesn't speak through proxies on the tabloid pages or feed ammo to his friends in the broadcast booth. Those were Steinbrenner ploys when Cashman and Torre were targets, reading about themselves in blind quotes. However incensed that stuff made him, Cashman never fired back. He knew you don't win arguments with a foghorn.

But Steinbrenner is gone now, dead for almost a decade, and Cashman did more than just survive him. While no one was looking, he created a team in his own image that looks and sounds nothing like George. His players take in data but give none of it out: they all speak the tongue of blank proverbs. Boone is a charmer who engages reporters while stiffing them for back-page fodder. There's a vast apparatus undergirding the team, but Cashman, who built that internal structure to his specifications, cloaks it in fuzzy math and vague descriptors. Out with King George and his cult of Trumpian carnage. In with organization and the strength of machine learning. *These* Yankees are a future that keeps arriving.

While he gradually grew power, Cashman found his second voice — and as those who've heard it know, it's a doozy. With no change of affect or a look to see who's listening, he'll toss a live grenade into casual conversation, jolt you with a story or a barbed aside. When Cashman's off the clock, he's a killer raconteur, telling tales on everyone, himself included. It's the last thing you look for from a monochrome guy who seems to have scrubbed his DNA of melatonin.

Everything about Cashman reeks of caution: the size of his desk, which is so expansive, it's like holding a conversation across a moat; his uniform of polos, dad-slacks, and boat shoes, which would place him comfortably behind a service desk at Best Buy; and his discomfort watching a game around other people, particularly at Yankee Stadium. As part of his deal, he gets a luxury suite that seats ten and is fully catered. But instead of sitting there, he hunkers in his office, catching the YES broadcast on TV. So situated, he can text to his heart's delight, trading squibs with scouts and quants around the country. The effect is of someone who is felt, not seen — a man who makes his mark, then disappears.

"Brian has the Colombo act down to a T, but he's got a dorsal fin under the water," says Oakland's Billy Beane, a longtime pal and admirer of Cashman's. "His mind is like a steel trap — the little bastard keeps notes on every conversation he's ever had, including with his *friends*. He'll say, 'You told me this in 2007' — and of course he's right."

When you earn Cashman's trust, you get treated to both his voices — occasionally in the same sentence. He'll be speaking in the first one, playing prevent defense, then suddenly drop into the second. One day you're asking about the build-out of his staff and getting nowhere fast on the subject. He can't (or won't) recall how many people he's hired, or how sharply he's grown his overhead. And then, without a blink, he'll tell you two stories, both of them decades old. The first concerns his own hiring in 1998 as the thirty-year-old GM of the New York Yankees. Per Cashman, the whole thing came as a rude shock: he'd nursed no aspirations to run the team. "If you'd worked for the Yankees and saw what I saw," he says, "the last thing you'd want is to be GM."

Bob Watson, the then-GM, had just stepped down and strongly recommended Cashman as his successor. Cashman begged Watson to reconsider, but no luck: a meeting with George was booked the next day. Cashman went home to his then-wife Mary and said, "This is the first day of my last days as a Yankee." Why? she asked, perplexed by his tone. "Because the next step is out the door," he said. "There's no other spot for me left."

Since joining the Yankees as a college intern in 1986, he'd watched George take apart powerful men who'd dared to fill the seat. "He brought in Syd Thrift from Pittsburgh and Bob Watson from Houston, guys who came with, *I saw him do that to others; he won't do it to me,*" says Cashman. "But I didn't go in there thinking, *How dare he do this to me?* I'd seen him do it to *everyone.*"

George wasted no time wooing Cashman at their Regency Hotel lunch. He told him he'd pay him a salary of $300,000 — a gross insult, even then — and said, "I could recycle someone who's done this before, but I've been told by too many people that you're capable." If nothing else, at least George's *timing* was rich. The Yankees were making their dynasty run, and '98 would be the jewel in their crown. They'd sweep the Padres for their second title in three years, smash the all-time mark for most wins in a season (125, including the playoffs), and spin the turnstiles at the old Yankee Stadium, drawing nearly three million for the first time. But Cashman, a compulsive praise-deflector, shuns any authorship of that team. "Gene Michael gets most of the credit, but he had nothing to do with the draft. The talent acquisition part was Brian Sabean and Bill Livesey: *they're* the reason we got Mariano, Jeter, and Pettitte and converted Posada from an infielder to catcher." The farm system they'd stocked was loaded with next-wave prospects, but "George whacked the guys" who drafted them. Sabean, Livesey, Kevin Elfering, Mitch Lukevics — "he took them all out because he had people in his ear saying they weren't any good." Sabean, of course, would go on to build *his* empire as the GM of the San Francisco Giants, but "he deserves a plaque here and some of Stick's credit," Cashman insists, for drafting and keeping the Core Four together.

The second story concerned Cashman's working conditions when George was running the show. In 1996, the Yankees finally broke through after decades in the baseball desert. They'd done nothing of interest since 1978, missed the playoffs outright for fourteen years, and become second-class citizens in their own town, losing New York to those brazen Mets teams of the 1980s. But now they were back, riding the star-child wave of Jeter, Pettitte, and Mo. That year they won the Eastern Division, beat the Orioles for the pennant (with a little divine intervention from a teenage fan named Jeffrey Maier), and stunned the lordly Braves in the World Series. It was bedlam the next morning in the Canyon of Heroes: seemingly half the city's census turned up on Lower Broadway to throw kisses and confetti at the Yanks. Even the Mets bent a knee in praise, buying an ad in the *Daily News* to congratulate the team and George himself. "I thought, *Wow, he must be on, like, cloud fucking nine if even the owner of the Mets is throwing bouquets*," says Cashman. Then Cashman rode downtown and found out different.

"As we pull into Battery Park and start getting off the bus, I hear just like this . . . *screaming* from George. He's red as a tomato, veins popping out of his neck, because the players are getting on floats with their wives." For Steinbrenner, wives were beneath contempt: they belonged on the bottom deck of the double-decker trolley that was driving behind the floats. "He's screaming at [Jim] Leyritz and [John] Wetteland, 'Get your fucking wives off the float!' The players are looking at their wives and looking at The Boss, and the wives are like, 'I'm going with my *husband!*'" So on the floats they went, and George turned his mortal wrath on poor Debbie Tymon, the team's event planner. "I was like, ah, *fugging ay,*" groans Cashman, reliving the moment. "If he's not happy after winning the World Championship, then there's nothing that will keep him happy — and I mean *nothing*."

For a while, you wonder why Cashman tells these stories. But by and by, a sense of a strategy looms: *he's actually guarding the safe while seeming to crack it.* His talking out of school about George and the past keeps listeners from drilling down in the present. Proud and proprietary toward this team, he won't let you look below the waterline. He raves, for instance, about his performance-science staff, then says, "Oh, by the way, they'll never talk to you, so don't even bother to ask." When asked about his mental-skills department, he pivots to the story of Chad Bohling.

Bohling is the creator and director of that staff, but Cashman's story about him is a smokescreen. Back in '98, when Cashman got the GM job, he interviewed Mark Shapiro to be his assistant. Shapiro, who's currently the president of the Jays, was a bright young thing then with the Cleveland Indians and was intrigued by the thought of joining the Yanks. As Cashman tells it, they were having lunch in Tampa when Shapiro asked if the Yanks had a mental-skills group. Cashman, who didn't, sorely wanted to start one, but knew better than to ask George for the money to do so. Then Shapiro asked the next question: Does George hand you a budget and let you spend it as you see fit? No, said Cashman, "Everything runs through George. He may green-light it one day, but if

Billy Connors gets in his ear, then the program's done." Connors was a member of the Tampa mob, a gifted pitching coach whom George had canned, then later hired as vice president. He reported to Mark Newman, then the director of player development, who ran the Yanks' fallow farm system. Together, they largely functioned to thwart the New York office, blocking all attempts to modernize. Hire additional scouts in the minors? *No.* Teach life skills to foreign-born prospects? *No.* Find Ivy League analysts to boost performance? *No, and stop asking, goddamnit!*

Though he desperately wanted to hire Shapiro as his ally, Cashman leveled with him. Shapiro declined the job but thanked Cashman for his candor. He would go on to become the two-time Executive of the Year as the builder of a title-winner in Cleveland. It was a bruising loss for Cashman that turned out to be a win: it confirmed his reputation as a truth-teller. "No one in this industry is closer to Brian than me, and one of the reasons he's so successful is, he's stand-up," says Omar Minaya, the ex-GM who built those vibrant Mets teams of the mid-2000s. Under George, "Cash wasn't able to make the moves he wanted, but he was always honest about it. For some guys, the word 'yes' never really meant 'yes.' Brian wasn't like that, and other GMs appreciated it."

With Shapiro, the reward was tangible: he wound up steering Cashman to Bohling. In 2005, "I almost left the Yankees," says Cashman, over the power struggle with Tampa. "But George says, 'I want you to stay. What will it take you to stay?' I said, 'I want to bring us into the new world order, starting with a mental-skills program.' He said, 'Fine, whatever you need, you'll do.'"

Cashman called Shapiro, who gave him five candidates. At the top of the list was Bohling, who had worked for Tom Coughlin while he ran the Jacksonville Jaguars. Cashman had direct-line access to Coughlin: he'd roomed with Coughlin's son Timmy when the two of them were young and just starting out in Manhattan. Coughlin confirmed that Bohling was brilliant, a sports-performance guru who gave raw prospects the psychic skills to advance. Beside teaching young players techniques to get through slumps, Bohling excelled at building team bonds — that gauzy but crucial thing called *chemistry*.

In the early to mid-2000s, the Yankees ruled the regular season but were bafflingly bad in October. They blew a ninth-inning lead in Game 7 against the D-backs in the 2001 World Series; lost the '03 World Series to the badly overmatched Marlins; and were the first team in baseball to gag a three-games-to-none lead in a best-of-seven series, self-destructing against the Red Sox in the infamous ALCS of 2004. They had power and pitching and the greatest closer of all time — but none of the closeness of the title-winning squads.

Their clubhouse had the feel of an off-site at the Hyatt. It was an assembly of well-paid strangers who'd been hired to boost profits and — at their soonest convenience — win a ring. The Core Four kids were now famous adults with competing corporate interests off the field. Surrounding them, boardroom style, were brand ambassadors brought in from other teams. Alex Rodríguez, Randy Johnson, Gary Sheffield, Kevin Brown, Mike Mussina, Jason Giambi, Raúl Mondesi: all were high achievers at their prior place of business but bad — or worse — style fits on this team. Even Giambi, who idolized Mickey Mantle and had dreamed all his life of being a Yankee, was hopelessly lost in that room. "He was a long-haired, Harley-riding, whiskey-drinking dude that George tried to ram in a square hole," says a team executive. "He made him cut his hair and get rid of the chopper — basically, made him someone that he wasn't." The close-cropped Giambi, a former AL MVP, struggled mightily at the plate in New York. He cranked a lot of homers his first two seasons, but was a .208 hitter by year three, when he was diagnosed with a pituitary tumor (which was subsequently treated without any complications). "We definitely messed him up, and I feel lousy about that; he was *such* a good guy," says the exec. "We thought it would go like [the trade for] Tino did, but for whatever reason, it never really did."

Tino, of course, is Tino Martinez, the previous star import at first base. As recounted earlier, he too was unnerved by the size of the town and the task. Then Torre took him aside, put an arm around his shoulder, and talked him through his bout of new-guy jitters. Those first five years — from 1996 to 2000 — Father Joe was the great confessor. He radiated kindness and a feel for those with troubles, having weathered his own maelstrom as a boy. (Torre witnessed his mother's beatings at the hands of his father, trauma he depicted in his memoir.) "He allowed you to work your way out of struggles — the fact that he had played made a difference," says Darryl Strawberry, who salvaged his career and reputation with the Yanks, hitting homers that helped win three World Series off the bench. "We had so many different types on our roster, but he made everyone feel important, and put us in the best position to succeed."

Alas, *that* Joe was all but gone by the time the Jason Giambi arrived. The extended triumph of the title years changed everyone on the club, Torre included. No longer was he managing twenty-five guys and making himself available to late arrivals. By then, "he didn't relate to the new guys at all — and I know that for a fact 'cause they complained," says a team official. "Torre had become Joe Corporate — he had Bigelow Tea and Chase in his office. He wasn't accessible to the Sheffields." For *his* part, Cashman hedged when asked if Torre's aloofness had cost the Yankees pennants. He was frank, however, about his displeasure with the outcomes. From 2001 to 2006, "we had championship-caliber teams that failed to finish," he says. "We entered the playoffs as odds-on favorites in Vegas, and for whatever reason didn't play well."

Those flameouts made Big Stein "*extremely*" upset," as he constantly told Torre through his touts. "He would have the YES Network embarrass Joe, ask him tough questions after losses," Cashman explains. Or George would "leak to Bill Madden at the *News* that he was secretly meeting with Lou Piniella to replace Torre." This was after the '06 playoffs, when the top-seeded Yanks lost without a whimper to the wild-card Tigers. It was yet another ouster in the divisional round, and this one was particularly bitter. When his powerhouse lineup didn't hit a lick, Torre seemed to single out Sheffield and A-Rod, benching one and batting the other eighth — or, "as Torre was saying then, 'double-cleanup,'" Cashman groans.

Still, Cashman fought on Joe's behalf when George tried to can Torre for Davey Johnson. "I remember going to bat to keep Joe here. I didn't think he warranted termination. We still were making the playoffs, hadn't bottomed out yet, which is generally what you do when you transition. Even in '07, when George decided to part ways, I asked him again to reconsider. But the money Joe was making, and the credit he took from George? George resented the *shit* out of that."

When asked to compare those late-Torre teams to the one in the locker room now, Cashman comes forward in his chair. "Oh, this team's chemistry's *off the charts*," he says, beaming. "That's a very unique group down there."

He declines to make the case with chapter and verse; like most GMs, he stays out of the clubhouse, respecting the authority of the manager. But Cashman has his sources in the locker room, and none are more important than Jason Zillo. Twelve years ago, when he decided to change the culture, Cashman enlisted Zillo, then the assistant media director, to groom and polish a better breed of Yankee. It was a long-term project that took years to bear fruit, in part because the system sent up so few prospects between the Core Four era and this one. Over that twenty-year span, only three homegrown hitters had enough at-bats for a batting title, and exactly four starters had logged enough innings to win an ERA crown.

Still, those lean years gave Zillo a lot of runway to road-test his training program. "The idea was to take kids like [Phil] Hughes and [Robby] Cano and teach them how to do it the right way when *they* became elder statesmen," says Zillo. Eventually, he hoped, they'd be his "feeder system," "good clubhouse guys" whom young players took after, starting "a snowball effect." Hughes and Cano were gone, of course, before they could spread the light, but by then Zillo had filled the pipeline with kids who behaved like Aaron Judge.

Zillo, forty-one now, runs a media shop that has doubled in size since he started. (Like Cashman, he joined the Yankees out of college and has worked for no one else as an adult.) A trim, affable chap who's built a lot like Cashman and seems to share a wardrobe with him, he is himself a model for these good-guy Yanks: accommodating and genial within set limits, someone whose game face is always on. He's set himself the task of bottling the Core Four's ethos and diffusing it at every level from A-ball up. That starts in the first few days of spring training: at both the major league camp at Steinbrenner Field and the instructional camp across the street, Zillo shows the players proprietary videos of how — or more like it, how *not* — to handle the New York press. Not surprisingly, the Yankees guard these videos like they were nuclear launch codes. Though the details can't be shared, the yield of seeing them can: The clips are surprisingly powerful. They're hilarious and graphic and discomforting to watch. No kid could view them without being scared straight on the risks of speaking his mind.

Conversely, the two clips *also* extol the virtues of being accountable to the press. If you screw up on the field, just own it and move on; don't deflect blame and make things worse. If asked a tough question about real-world matters, be polite but decline the invitation. (It happens. If you're a public figure in this age of atrocities, someone's going to ask you about mass shootings.) After the videos run, the Yankees turn the floor over to a different guest speaker every year. Last spring, it was A-Rod, whose media history reads like *War and Peace*. Yes, the same A-Rod who sued the commissioner of baseball, then turned around and sued the Yankees' team physician, was now fielding questions from impressionable kids on the right way to put out fires. Zillo notes about A-Rod: "He was honest with the guys about his own mistakes—and I *promise* you they were paying strict attention."

These days every club does some kind of media training, but the Yankees, who got there first, work it harder. Apart from team sessions, they stage role-play workshops for kids with less than four years of service. "We'll get three or four players to play media members, give them mikes and cameras" and a hot-button topic to pose to a chosen teammate. Gun rights, immigration—the reporters dig deep, making the players "super-nervous and sweaty." In 2017, they pressed a Latino prospect for his feelings about Trump's proposed wall. "Afterwards, we debriefed him," says Zillo, "and he's like, 'My heartbeat was going—I cried so many nights, not having my family here.'" There aren't a lot of clubs devoting off-days in March to live-fire media drills, but as Cashman said, it's better to have guardrails at the top than an ambulance waiting at the bottom. The yield of all that training is a single-minded squad that speaks with one voice in public. Play back any postgame interview last year. No matter who the Yankee is, his tactic is the same: *Talk about the team, not yourself.*

Typically, the chink in a club's messaging chain is the top-ranked prospect who's been promoted. He's had all eyes on him since he was drafted out of high school or signed overseas at sixteen, and that blend of jock swagger and peak naïveté can land him, wheels up, in a ditch. How often have you seen a kid come in and lose the locker room in an eyeblink? Whether it's Gregg Jefferies, who was such a diva that he demanded the Mets ship his bats separately from the teams', then wound up fishing them out of a trash can after Strawberry dumped them in a rage; or Noah Syndergaard, whose lunch was snatched by David Wright when he elected to eat it during a preseason game — you only get one chance to make a bad impression that follows you around the league. But not the Yankees — not anymore. One after another, they bring up polished products who say and do *everything* right.

On the fourth Sunday in April, when they were barely above water and floundering behind Boston and the Jays, the Yanks promoted Gleyber Torres, the Hope diamond of their vaunted system. A kid from Venezuela acquired from the Cubs in Cashman's benchmark heist of 2016 (the reliever he gave up, Aroldis Chapman, signed back with the Yankees that fall), Torres was twenty-one and had half a season's experience of high-minors ball for the Yanks. A born shortstop, he was also playing out of position: blocked by Gregorius, he'd been shunted to second, where he was still doing on-the-job training. But for a chunk of the '18 season, he was the Yanks' best all-around player, a kid with the advanced skill set and emotional savvy of a ten-year star.

Boone batted him ninth to break him in easy and add a little length to the lineup. Instead, Torres took the team off Didi's shoulders and carried it for the next five weeks. Between April 24 and June 4, no one could get him out. He hit .336, drove in twenty-seven runs, and almost broke the record for fastest-to-ten-homers by a Yankees rookie. None of those shots were short-porch chippies: the kid who hadn't hit for power in the minors was launching them to the black in dead-center. In a stretch when most of the run producers were mired in long funks (Stanton, Sánchez, and Gregorius hit .211 combined and were benched off and on by Boone), Torres and Miguel Andújar, the rookie costars, turned the batting order upside down.

Those five weeks made the Yankees' season. They played .750 ball, overtook the Sox, and became the team everyone feared back in March. During a particularly grueling run against the league's best clubs — from late April to May 10, the Yanks played thirteen games against the Angels, Astros, Indians, and Red Sox and won eleven of them — Torres was the difference-maker. One four-day span largely told the tale: the kid was a born killer in big spots. On May 3, against the Astros on the final lap of their Western trip, the Yankees were down 5–3 in the ninth, after a rare blown save by Chad Green. Torres, a marvelous two-strike hitter, short-stroked a 3-2 slider to deep left, tying the game and sending the go-ahead run to third; Judge delivered that runner, one out later, with a grounder.

The next night Torres sparked his dog-tired team with a three-run bomb to left, jumping them out to an early lead on Cleveland. Two days later, after another bullpen bobble, this one by Dellin Betances, the ice-cold Stanton was intentionally walked so the Indians could face Torres in the ninth. He fought off slider after slider to get to 3-2, then jumped at a changeup on the outer half. The ball leapt off his barrel, bound for right-center, but just kept going and going. By the time it fell to earth in the Yankees' pen, 415 feet the opposite way, the huge Sunday crowd had gone berserk. As the Indians trudged off, wondering what had hit them, and the Yankees hopped the rail to dog-pile Torres, Didi grabbed the Gatorade bucket and drenched him not once but twice. Soaked to the skin, Torres calmly wiped his face and fielded questions from on-field reporters. In lilting but broken English, he chanted the catechism: *I try stay focus and help the team.*

Afterwards, in the deafening *boom-bap!* clubhouse, Marcus Thames, the hitting coach, talked about Torres, whom he'd mentored the prior off-season. Torres was in Tampa rehabbing his elbow, having torn it on a head-first slide at Triple-A. They were training in baseball's dead-zone — that five-week stretch between Thanksgiving and New Year's Eve — and Torres could have easily mailed it in, doing drills and some light lifting before flying home. Instead, he obsessed over every detail: weight shift and launch path and pitch recognition, endlessly pumping Thames for information. Out of nowhere one day he brought up Dallas Keuchel, the Astros' lefty who'd owned the Yanks for years. "I study him in the World Series," he said to Thames. "You gotta take what he give to you and go to right field on him."

Thames was stunned. Most players don't watch the Series: it's too painful to bear if you're not in it. But here was a twenty-year-old, four months postsurgery, who'd treated it like a night school course. He'd already gleaned that there were pitchers like Keuchel who never give in to a hitter, throwing him further and further away until he submits and rolls a grounder to short. "It said a lot about his maturity and awareness," says Thames. "You don't see that stuff in a rookie." Six months later, in May, Torres went up against Keuchel and hunted for a pitch to drive. Ultimately, Keuchel hung a slider to him; Torres scorched it into the corner for a double. After the inning ended, he passed Thames in the dugout. "Remember what we talked about in Tampa?" he said, winking.

Torres was named Rookie of the Month for May and, through June, was the early runaway favorite to win the Rookie of the Year Award. His only competitors were the Angels' Shohei Ohtani and Miggy Andújar, his lineup mate. But Andújar, who was promoted weeks earlier by the Yanks, ran a full length behind him in production. On the field, the two rookies played like twins; off it, they were nothing alike. Andújar, a kid from the Dominican tropics, walked around the clubhouse with an incandescent grin, as if he couldn't quite credit his good luck. He played cards with his Latin teammates, shimmied to bachata, and dressed like he had a date with a ring-card girl.

Torres, on the other hand, was pensive to the point of silence, sitting and staring at his cell phone. He hails from Caracas, a city so sunk in dystopian chaos that even soldiers stay in after dark there. It's the murder capital of the hemisphere, a place where killings go unreported and clans with any cash are kidnap targets. Every morning Torres texts his mother and father to see how they got through the night. Before and after games, he pings Elizabeth, his young wife, who came over in 2018 to join him in New York. "There is trouble there," he tells us. "I ask, 'Is everything all right?' and they tell me they are fine, just focus on baseball."

For Torres, that's easier said than done. His country, like the Dominican Republic, is baseball-crazy, and his exploits make him back-page gold. More than 350 of his countrymen have gotten to the bigs; several are in the Hall of Fame, or bound there soon enough, including Luis Aparicio, José Altuve, and Miguel Cabrera. "Everyone is paying attention to Gleyber, he's on the news there every night," says his teammate and countryman Ronald Torreyes. "People are proud of him, especially since he's playing for the Yankees, who are very popular in my country."

It wasn't just Venezuelans who took notice. None other than Roberto Alomar, a native Puerto Rican and Hall of Fame second baseman, started making mental notes of Torres even when Gleyber was a low-level minor leaguer. Alomar, currently a Blue Jays adviser, was gathering data on Toronto's prospects back in 2016 and began homing in on the Tampa Yankees' fiery little infielder.

Torres, only nineteen at the time, had just been traded to the Yankees from the Cubs in the Aroldis Chapman deal. He was a stranger to the Florida State League and had no reason to believe a legend would be watching him from the stands. Nevertheless, he put on a show. "[Gleyber] reminded me a lot of myself in the way he played the game and carried himself," Alomar said. "I mean, I was quicker than him, but he had more power. You could see he was smiling, he was happy. You could tell he loved baseball. I was thinking, 'Gleyber is me when I was a kid.'"

The two finally met in 2018 in person, although under much different circumstances. By then Torres had crushed his audition in the

Bronx, but June was exacting its toll on the rookie. Torres's average fell eighty points; his OPS was down by almost a third. Opposing pitchers were beating him with inner-half heat, sensing Torres's bat was a tick slower. That was the surcharge he was now paying for those early-season home runs. Torres was so conscious of maintaining that long-ball swing that he only managed to gum up his fast-twitch muscles.

Slumps are a near-prophecy for most hotshots. Typically, it's the domain of the team's hitting instructor and a wise veteran to help the kid work through the baggage. But Yankees president Randy Levine had another idea: he reached out to Ray Negron, the Yankees' community relations adviser, knowing he and Alomar were close friends. Could Alomar help? Would he? It was a bold, back-channel request, a member of the Blue Jays' organization performing triage on a Yankee, but Alomar was already saying "yes" before Negron had finished asking. He hadn't forgotten the young star on Tampa's back fields.

Alomar and Torres met informally in the theater district one Saturday evening in June, just before Torres and his wife were about to enter the Minskoff Theatre to see *The Lion King*. Alomar had other plans that night, but arranged for a few critical minutes outside the box office. There, he and Torres, speaking in Spanish, broke down the slump. More importantly, Alomar sought to restore Torres's wavering confidence.

"I knew Gleyber was struggling. I'd watched enough Yankees games to see that," Alomar said by telephone one day this past November. "I made two points to him. The first was about concentration and dedication. I said, 'Anyone can be good, but to be great you have to be married to this game.'"

Alomar then paused to make a second salient point to Torres, who listened in rapt attention. "I told him, 'Hitting is a lot like throwing a ball: your hands have to go back before you can throw to first base. You have to wind up. It works the same way in hitting. Your front knee has to go back towards your bat, and *then* you go forward. That's where your power comes from.'"

What Alomar had been seeing from Torres was markedly different.

"Gleyber's front leg was going straight up, not back," Alomar said. "He was straight and narrow, which meant he was going forward without power. He was worried about getting jammed, but I said, 'You're beating yourself, you're slow in the zone. If you have confidence in your legs, you'll come back.' And he did."

Despite a minor hip injury, Torres raised his average in each of the next two months. But few in the clubhouse ever knew about the meeting with Alomar; Torres shields his privacy fiercely. He never gossips, especially about himself. His personal bio line in the Yankees' media guide is eight words long. Each night he goes home and double-bolts the door, never joining teammates for an evening out. When he was DL'ed last year, he worked so diligently on his English that he now declines an interpreter when he speaks. Still, he talks only to a handful of teammates. One of them is Didi, who brought him under his wing and counseled him on the importance of on-field conduct. Torres plays with an edge that verges on arrogance: he has a habit of challenging home-plate umps over borderline ball/strike calls. These Yankees don't do stare-downs, least of all by rookies. Politeness matters to a patient team that takes as many pitches as they do. "I was a very young player like him once," Didi tells us when we ask about his advice to Torres. "He doesn't need me to take care of him — he's pretty confident already — but I'm there if he wants it."

Time was — like, three years ago — a rookie came up and said nothing to the umps till he'd earned his bones. Not anymore. In the post-juice era, the game's swung so hard in the direction of youth that rookies now have leverage, and they use it. It's common to see Juan Soto, the twenty-year-old man-child, linger at the plate to admire his bombs, or

Ronald Acuña, the swag-a-licious slugger, spurn a $30 million exten-
sion *before his call-up*. If they incense their veteran teammates, well,
hey, *whatevs* — they'll be around long after those sourpuss geezers are
gone. The upshot is that it's dicey for a manager to draw the line with
player decorum: he can easily freeze relations with a rising star by over-
playing his hand.

One day in the summer of 2018, Willie Randolph, the great ex-Yankee who managed the Mets to the brink of the World Series in '06, was
talking about a run-in he'd had with José Reyes that presaged the coming shift in power relations. On the eve of their NLCS against the Cardinals that fall, Randolph held an informal workout at Shea Stadium.
Reyes, wearing a do-rag in lieu of his cap, was waiting to take his turn
in the batting cage. It was a small thing, but Randolph pulled him aside
and told him to go in and get his hat. "I was trying to build camaraderie,
instill the idea that we're one and do everything as a team." Reyes, then
twenty-three but already an All-Star shortstop, gave his manager "*that*
look" before heading in. "He was pouting and didn't like it," said Randolph, adding that if "I had it to do over, I wouldn't've done it that way.
I didn't take into account how the younger guys react; it's a different
generation these days."

As the Yankees learned the hard way with Gary Sánchez last year, you
don't go at a sensitive kid head-on. Instead, you dispatch your biggest
star to quietly have a word with him. At the start of June, Torres's great
run ended. He got homer-happy and began leaving the zone, chasing
high heat and sliders away. The strikeouts began to gnaw at him; for
the first time in the bigs, he was flailing. One day, as he was coming off
back-to-back oh-fers, Aaron Judge put an arm around his waist. Bend-
ing slightly to be heard above the clatter of their cleats, Judge did all the
talking in a terse half-whisper while they walked from the dugout to
the clubhouse.

Through no accident whatsoever, the Yankees gave Torres the stall beside Judge's on the left-hand wall. Looking around to make sure that he wasn't being spied on, Judge kept talking sotto voce. He made a gesture with his palms, the yogic injunction to *Relax; stay the course; let it go.* Torres's shoulders softened as he listened, nodding. For the first time in weeks, he looked like what he was: a kid barely old enough for a beer. Behind his reserve, there's a sweetness in Torres that comes through when he feels acknowledged. You can see it on the field after he's had a big hit: he casts a shy grin in the direction of the dugout, as if searching for his parents in the stands. Those are the kinds of moments when baseball rings heroic: a young man making his mark, and his new tribe taking him in. That's why the game still matters to adults who fell for it early in life. At bottom, it's always about coming home, wherever the road wound after you left.

For Judge too, that moment was a kind of arrival. He didn't ask to be the leader of the world's most lustrous team; rather, it was thrust upon him by his stature. For longer than it knows, baseball has yearned for Aaron Judge, a star whose unfakeable, bone-deep goodness resonates through the screen. He is that rarest thing in sports: a gentleman-soldier committed to the men in his ranks. Endorsements? Very few. Cover stories? Sorry, no time now, he tells everyone — through Zillo, who handles the requests for him.

In the summer of Judge's rookie season, Bob Klapisch got an hour alone with him and found him puzzled by his fame. At the time, he was leading the world in homers, the Stadium was packed with girls in peek-a-boo ALL RISE tops, and there was a line of reporters waiting for a word with him. He answered Bob's questions with gracious evasions, weighing the right to ask them against his right to self-concealment. He didn't resent the attention exactly, but saw no point in fanning it. One exchange during that chat was telling: when asked if he noticed the MARRY ME! signs being flashed in the right-field stands, Judge flushed slightly and gave his gap-toothed grin. "I'm twenty-five," he said, "and

I've got ten years to accomplish what I want to in this game. When I'm thirty-five, maybe I'll give that stuff some thought, but . . ."

And here he was now, almost exactly a year later, giving life advice to a lonely, fretful kid. Asked a week or so later what he'd said to Torres to help him through his slump, Judge fixed Klapisch with a measuring gaze. He has a habit of filing away little surprises for further contemplation. "Nothing much, you know: 'Just keep your head up,'" he said. "'Everyone goes through it, but you're great and we're gonna need you, so, you know, hang with it.'"

Several weeks later, there was another notch moment in the ascension of Aaron Judge. The Yankees had just rallied for a rousing win against a red-hot Mariners team. Down 5–0 to old friend Félix Hernández, they came all the way back to tie it in the bottom of the eighth on a two-run homer by Sánchez. The game seemed ticketed for extra innings when Stanton came up in the ninth. Looking for a two-out pitch to end it, he caught an 0-2 hanger and bludgeoned it off the facing of the center-field bleachers. It was one of those Stanton blasts that felt like an unpacking—a purge of expectations, and the weirdness of playing second fiddle to Judge.

They lockered at opposite ends of a wall: Judge in a cubicle close to the front door, Stanton on the far side by the exit. Stanton, the new guy nervous around writers, could quietly slip out after a game without having to take extra questions. Judge, on the other hand, had to walk a gauntlet to get to the parking lot. Every five feet, he was stopped by a reporter with "one last thing" to ask. (Judge being Judge, he always obliged.) And style-wise, the two stars were planets apart. Stanton, an *extremely* active bachelor, dressed like a James Bond villain. He wore exquisite blazers of complex fabrics over silk-and-viscose V-necks snugged to fit. Judge, the don't-care hunk, rocked hoodies and jeans, as if headed for a slice-and-a-beer across the street. If they ever stopped to chat, you didn't see it at the park. Their clubhouse is the size of a hotel lobby, and they seemed content to give each other space and let time and opportunity bring them closer.

On this particular night, though — after his homer beat the Mariners — Stanton was the last one dressed, so mobbed was he by reporters. Almost unseen, Judge hung at his locker, waiting for the writers to leave. When they finally cleared the room, he ambled by Stanton's locker. As they walked out together, he clapped him on the back and did a little shimmy in celebration. It wasn't much to look at, but he let out a war whoop as he did it. Stanton cracked up, one of those full-body laughs that's equal parts levity and relief. *Thank you*, his grin seemed to say to Judge. *Thank you, man. And yes: I'm home.*

4

AN AUDIENCE IN THE JUDGE'S CHAMBERS

Two months into the season, the book on these Yankees was that they were going to grind you down. Series after series, they'd beaten the best clubs in baseball by methodically crushing their will. Their hallmark trait was relentlessness: they followed long at-bat with long at-bat till they sapped the strength of opposing staffs. Expected to throw bombs like an early Tyson, their lineup proved much more vintage Ali — probing and patient as it tracked its foe, waiting for an opening to present. Often, they spent the first five innings hunting for a hanger. If they didn't get it, they were fine taking a called strike three after a seven- or eight-pitch stare-down.

The toll that ploy took was mental as much as anything. An opposing starter knew he was being stalked by pursuers who could smell his exhaustion from sixty feet. The second he flagged, the Yankees were on him in numbers, busting open games with late rallies. The Yanks didn't panic if they trailed after five or if their starter tossed a clunker; they led the world in wins in their last at-bat. No other team in baseball could make a nine-inning game feel like the Thrilla in Manila.

That's a terrific way to operate in the regular season, when the weeks come at you in a deathless blur and you don't get to catch your breath until October. But October is a whole different game. There are two days off in a playoff series, when starters are only tasked to throw five innings, then turn things over to rested pens. Inversely, each start is magnified: if you fall behind early against a team with strong relief, you can watch your season end in five days. The Yankees, of course, had the bullpen covered; what they lacked, after Severino, was a second ace. So it didn't feel presumptuous, a third of the way into the season, to ask Cashman how he hoped to redress that.

Sitting in his office at the end of May, he was asked — and asked again — how much he was prepared to pay for a Jacob deGrom or a Blake Snell. They'd be freakishly dear in terms of talent surrendered, costing, at minimum, three blue chips apiece and probably a major leaguer tossed in. Still, the Yanks had such a glut of riches that they could afford to overpay. They had the stock, for instance, to revive the rudderless Mets by sending them three or four players who, come 2020, would be the drive train of a compelling team. And for deGrom at least, no surcharge seemed unreasonable: by the All-Star break, he was the best arm in baseball. An exceptionally young thirty in terms of wear and tear, he'd never pitched a day of competitive ball until his junior year of college. Almost twenty-six when he reached the bigs, he'd just now rounded into his prime and would be under Mets' control through 2020. If the price for him was Andújar and three strong prospects, well, the return was a live chance to win a couple of titles before deGrom hit the free-agent market.

But as forthcoming as he was about the past, Cashman would give up nothing about the future. He parried questions by praising his own starters, then grudgingly mused that he *might* deal for Madison Bumgarner if he could live with the price. "I mean, if it's Bumgarner for Gleyber, we're not doing it." On deGrom, though, he squashed the notion fast. Relations were so bad with the Mets' ownership group that Cashman wouldn't discuss it *off* the record. Clearly, nothing was going to happen between the Yanks and deGrom until he hit free agency in 2020.

Regarding talks for other teams' pitchers, Cashman had one limit from his owner: he couldn't add a salary that put the Yankees over the luxury tax threshold of $197 million in 2018. No news there: he'd been under the same restriction since at least the '15 season. The news was that there was no *friction* there: about budgets, Cashman and Hal are in full alignment. They loathe throwing good money after bad at players. Doing so is an affront to both men's values. "I used to tease Cash about it — that he secretly wanted to run the Yankees the way we run the A's," says Beane. "Deep down, he hated George's business model. He knew there was no way to outspend teams forever and just wanted to be efficient."

Efficiency, to men like Cashman, means dealing with anyone who offers the best return — even if that anyone is Boston. "I'd've traded Andrew Miller to the Red Sox [in '16] if they'd sniffed on it," says Cashman. "But they didn't, and they needed bullpen help. The Mets too, but they didn't sniff on it either, which I thought was odd." How differently might the postseason have played that year had the Mets acquired Miller, the unhittable lefty? To be sure, they wouldn't have sent out Jeurys Familia to torch their wild-card game against the Giants; he served up a three-run bomb in the ninth to wreck Noah Syndergaard's two-hit gem. In fact, the fates of four teams seemed to turn on two trades: Chapman to the Cubs, not the Washington Nationals, and Miller to the Indians, not the Mets. The Cubs and Indians played a Series for the ages, with Chapman and Miller pitching their hearts out in that immortal Game 7 seesaw. The Mets and Nationals were sent home early, having missed their main chance at a title. Both teams are now in deep decline, passed in their division by the Braves and threatened by the Phillies, who looked in the mirror and started over. There's a lesson in their rebirth: *know thyself.* Win-

ning teams grasp and own their failures; losing teams are owned by
their failures.

But if you're going to talk efficiency with these Yankees, the conversation begins with Hal Steinbrenner. In 2008, when Hal was approved as
the general managing partner of the New York Yankees, no one foresaw
the paradigm shift he'd implement as team leader. To the extent that
anyone had a read on him, he was viewed, at thirty-nine, as a reluctant
heir, the son who didn't appear to love the game or have his father's fire
in the belly. His brother Hank was thought to be the inevitable choice:
he was loud and somewhat crude and liked regaling the press. Hank
briefly became the voice of the team when George took ill in 2007. Hal,
meanwhile, tended to the hotel chain that he'd built with a partner in
Florida and spent his free time practicing takeoffs and landings in his
Cessna high-wing. With his master's in business and abhorrence of
bunkum, he was perfectly happy being the Steinbrenner no one heard
from outside of boardroom meetings.

In 2008, Randy Levine was summoned to Tampa to help Big Stein
settle on a successor. Levine, the team president and George's consigliere, had done much of the heavy lifting in creating the YES Network and wrangling tax breaks to build the new Stadium. "George told
me, 'Talk to everyone in the family. See who *they* think should do this,
then get back to me.'" Levine sat with George's children and his wife,
Joan; the unanimous choice was Hal. "I went back to George, who said,
'That's where I would've gone too,'" says Levine.

Hal set himself the task of learning the baseball business from the
gatehouse up. For much of the '09 season, he stayed out of his office,
studying each department and its staff. "He put his arms around the
guts of the organization, listening to everyone in the building and the
booth," says Levine. Hal went to the owners' meetings and cultivated

Bud Selig, the then-commissioner with whom his dad had once done battle. Struck by his seriousness, Selig put him on the committee that handled collective bargaining with the players. (Selig's successor, Rob Manfred, would later promote Hal to baseball's executive council.) An incrementalist, Hal wasn't ready to make bold changes or quash the Yanks' pursuit of pricey stars. They were winning their division and printing money at the gate, even after their flameouts in the playoffs. But he was a businessman who believed in data sets and the efficiencies of thrift. When he ran the numbers at season's end, he saw nothing to suggest that spending $200 million was a passkey to a title. After the Yankees won their rings in 2009, the next three champions had an average payroll of approximately $106 million.

Then, in 2013, the bottom fell out of his $230 million team. That group of brittle stars and scrap-yard fill-ins suddenly hit the rocks and missed the playoffs. As the Red Sox romped to a third title in ten years, the Yanks limped in with a weak finish, fielding immortals like David Adams and Zoilo Almonte. It wasn't quite the capsize of the Horace Clarke years, but it was clear that the Big Stein model had run aground. With wealth redistribution and random drug-testing of players, you could no longer rig a winner with your wallet. Between luxury taxes and revenue-sharing, the Yankees were paying more than $100 million a year to scrappy young comers like the Royals. Meanwhile, the teams Hal sent out there now were all but unwatchable. They weren't just dull and unathletic — they were *irrelevant,* the jock version of *Cats.* "It felt like we were playing in front of tourists," says David Robertson, the good-guy veteran reliever. "They were visitors who were told, 'You must see Yankee Stadium,' but weren't even baseball fans."

What was needed was a teardown, but the Yankees don't do those; the cold gaze of their history forbids it. Instead, they'd have to try something so complex that no one had ever seen it before: a complete reinvention of their business model *while doing business as usual*. No three-year tank jobs for a higher draft choice or fire sales of veteran assets — this team had to keep signing up stars even as it spent to grow its own. It was like running a Michelin three-star restaurant as you renovate the kitchen, except the guests aren't supposed to taste the sawdust. You can pull it off only if you have *great* bags of money and an owner willing to wince and write huge checks.

Over the next three seasons, Hal spent to patch the roster while funding Cashman's overhaul of the innards. "Everything I asked for — a performance science department, a second academy in the DR — he said yes to," says Cashman. Those "patches," it's worth noting, would have panicked other owners: in total, the signings of Tanaka, McCann, Carlos Beltrán, and Jacoby Ellsbury cost $458 million. What Hal got for all his lucre was a plausible hedge: teams that won eighty-something games a year and nosed around a wild card till September. "He felt an obligation to the folks who loved this team: we had to stay competitive till the kids came," says Levine.

Meanwhile, there were other fires for Hal to fight: a year-over-year crash in viewership on YES and a double-digit drop in home attendance. Middle-class fans — cops, firefighters, and the like — were melting away and weren't being replaced by their kids. "We lost between seven and eight thousand season-ticket holders, the people buying thirty- or forty-game plans, and the generation behind them wasn't buying," says Levine. Hal paid for studies to see what millennials wanted when they came to a game. One of the things he learned was that, for many of them, the game was incidental. Instead, they went for the *experience* of watching a game and to document that experience on Snapchat and Facebook in the story they told friends about their lives. So informed, Hal spent millions resetting the stage. He converted the concourse overlooking Monument Park into an enormous outdoor bar and built selfie stations, with strategic backdrops, all around the park. He gave ticket-package buyers pregame access to the field, where they could take pictures of themselves posing with players. Lastly, Hal created a social media staff to blog each pitch of the game. Ten years ago, there were only writers in the press box. Now the beat writers are vastly outnumbered by twenty-something nerds posting the action.

But set-dressing the park didn't change the fact that the Yanks were a blah production. Tanaka and company were underperforming, Judge and Sánchez hadn't arrived yet, and Cashman's hands were tied by bloated contracts. Barring an act of God, they'd have to burn off those deals, be a team that didn't contend for three years. They'd win eighty-plus games a season while working in some kids and keeping their powder dry for Machado and Harper. If all went according to plan, they'd be back in 2019 with a dynasty built of phenoms and free agents.

Except, in 2016, fortune broke their way, jumping the development timeline. Two teams without a title in living memory were contenders in need of closers. Sensing irrational exuberance in the Indians and Cubs, Cashman approached Hal for permission to back the truck up. He wanted to sell more than just Chapman and Miller into the teeth of a red-hot market: he had three position players (McCann, Beltrán, and Castro) who could fetch a bounty of kids. But Hal put his hand up: McCann and Castro were off the table, and no deals for the relievers could be transacted unless they were replaced by veteran arms. Hal wasn't about to scrub one season, let alone three; he had an ethical pact to honor with the fans.

His temperance proved prescient. Cashman got his historic haul, including Torres, Clint Frazier, Dillon Tate, and Justus Sheffield—plus major league relievers in Adam Warren and Tyler Clippard. The Yankees brought up Sánchez and Judge, went on a tear that almost won them the wild card, and set the scene for their unexpected run in 2017.

Cashman later peeled off Castro and McCann in subsequent winter deals. The net return for them: Giancarlo Stanton.

To be sure, mistakes were made along the way. Three times the Yankees passed on great pitchers over the course of a calendar year. In the winter of '16, they let Chris Sale go to the Red Sox without a fight. At the deadline in '17, they left Justin Verlander to the clutches of the Houston Astros. That winter they let the Astros grab Gerrit Cole to pair with Verlander and Charlie Morton. Cashman, who has acquired one impact starter (Sabathia) since nicking Roger Clemens in '99, buys off the rack when shopping for arms. Jeff Weaver, Cory Lidle, Nate Eovaldi — none of them were special when he picked them up, and none were any better as Yankees. Off history alone, he should have bucked his gut and made the play for Verlander; instead, he honored Hal's directive to keep the payroll flat.

Still, Hal's rebuild was a smash success — and no one saw him do it. Rather, he deflected credit to Cashman when he spoke at the owners' meetings, one of the only times all year Hal agrees to talk. In stealth mode, the product of old-boy Williams College had effectively launched a tech firm that played baseball. Every inch of his Yankees was newly digitized, from TrackMan guns that gauge a teenager's spin rate to data on how the kid fields a ball thrown below his knees. He'd sunk millions into the A-ball complex in Tampa, financed the build-out of Cashman's data staff, and hired the largest corps of pro and amateur scouts in all of major league baseball. Counterintuitively, his motive was cost containment.

Since 2002, when baseball imposed levies on teams that overspent, New York had paid out $340 million to small-market clubs in luxury taxes. In 2014, the Yankees spent $260 million and missed the playoffs by four games. In 2018, they spent $190 million on the third-best record in baseball. For the first time in decades, they were under the limit — and making money faster than they could count it. Attendance was back where it was in 2012, up 18 percent in two years; the ratings on YES beat *broadcast* numbers and reversed the losses of the lean years; and Judge and Stanton jerseys, two of the top sellers in the sport, blanketed the grandstands.

You could feel and hear the difference at the Stadium: the crowd was a verbal menace again. Back in the old joint, the noise and abuse punked even the grizzled Red Sox. Those old-school plumbers and welders came spoiling for fights, screaming their lungs out at players in road grays before brawling with the guys in the next row. That belligerence went missing when the new park opened and the lunch-pail types stayed away; millennials only fight on Instagram. But when the Baby Bombers showed up, so did the meatheads. "The hardened fans are back," says Dave Robertson. "They're rowdy, and it makes a difference."

Come the sixth or seventh inning of a one-run game, there's a tremor in the home half of the frame. It starts beneath your feet — the concrete rumbles as though the D train were clattering by. If the Yankees get a man on, half the crowd stands; the other half rises if Judge is up. It is hard to think of a bond between a player and a park like the one Judge has forged in the Bronx. Walk the promenade, where fans mill before games underneath the giant bat. The firemen with farm tans driving F-150s with TRUMP/PENCE bumper stickers; the kids from the block rocking Boricua tats and something thin and shiny around their neck; the finance brahs in checked Bermudas squiring hot numbers from the office — they're all draped in Judge regalia, and some of them (too many) wear the stupid wig. Their projections onto Judge are peculiar to their tribe. The Trumpsters prize his power and politeness as tokens of a team-first past. The kids from the suburbs see one of their own, a backpacker dude of indeterminate race who might have skated ramps with their older sibs. And for fans of color, he's their everything: a multiethnic hero in a white man's sport; a boundary-busting star like The Rock or Vin Diesel; and the first brother to give the Yanks some swag since the arrival of Reggie Jackson. When Stanton whiffs four times, fans boo him off the field. When Aaron Judge does it, they curse the ump for stretching the strike zone on him.

But when Judge gets ahold of one — oh good Lord, better grab something firm for support. For the second or two it takes the ball to leave his bat and complete its whip-crack ride to the seats, the whole place seems to lift off its pins, then drop back down with a thud. There's a sound that follows, a great gust of joy that feels like the release of something caged. One moment you're at a staid baseball game; the next you're at a rave in Majorca. Everywhere you look, people are on their feet dancing, twirling, and bouncing with hands overhead and dapping up the stranger three seats down. It's the damnedest thing to watch — and it happens all the time. In each of his full seasons, Judge clocked twice as many homers at home as on the road. A fair number of those shots either started or capped a comeback against their pennant rivals.

Consider one seven-week sequence in '18. On May 9, he crushed a two-run shot to key a rally against the Red Sox in the eighth; with the win, the Yankees tracked down Boston to land in a first-place tie. On May 12, he hit another two-run bomb to help flush a big deficit to the A's. On May 29, it was Houston's turn: his moon-launch to right brought the Yankees back in a game they'd steal in the tenth. On June 21, he iced down Seattle with a two-run blast off James Paxton. At the time, Paxton was pitching like a young Chris Sale for a Mariners team nipping at Houston's heels. They left town in shambles after a three-game sweep and never seriously threatened the Astros again. Then, on July 1, Judge ambushed David Price with a shock-and-awe drive to dead-center. Price, the sometimes snowflake who'd pissed off all of Boston but whose left arm was critical to its chances, had finally gotten his act together and won eight of nine previous starts.

So much for hope: Judge's missile in the first snatched the heart out of Price's chest. Three batters later, Torres crushed one out to right, scoring Stanton and Didi ahead of him. Before Price knew it, he was down 8–0 in front of a national audience on Sunday night. It was one of those beatdowns that either defines a pitcher or corroborates old suspicions. Since joining the Sox in '16 as a max free agent, Price had been mugged for his lunch in the Bronx. Over five starts there, his aggregate line read: twenty-five innings pitched; forty-seven hits allowed; twenty-eight earned runs; ten homers. Judge's bomb that day confirmed a hard truth for Boston: come the playoffs, someone else would have to pitch game 2 here. Their second-best starter wasn't up to it.

An interview with Judge during that stretch was essential — and next to impossible to land. As noted earlier, it's increasingly hard to get one-on-ones with stars; with Judge, it's well nigh impossible. He has no publicist, no booker, and no discernible interest in the mechanics of personal branding. Here's a kid earning the minimum in the bigs who refuses to devote a minute to the swag chase that has convulsed other prodigies before him. There's no building-size shrine to him by Nike in Times Square, as there once was of the young Doc Gooden; no Head and Shoulders spots pummeling cable viewers, as there was with Odell Beckham Jr. For the first time in memory, fans could get to know an icon at a pace that felt proper to both parties. That may be one of the reasons people love Judge so fiercely: they see that he isn't in this for the fast buck and a cobranding hookup with Cardi B. In fact, if there's any life or love in Aaron Judge's love life, it really hasn't turned up much on TMZ. Everybody wants to ask him about *that* too — not whom he's dating, but how he's kept it to himself. But Judge is monkish in his dealings with the press.

On a steam-bath afternoon at Progressive Field in Cleveland, Klapisch sat with him in the dugout before a game. As with Stanton, it is hard to gauge the scale of Judge until he looms before you. In his nonchalant perfection, he seems to hail from a future where *everyone* has biceps as big as grapefruit and is drily indifferent to heat. Normal people sweat through their shirts in heat like this, but Judge was as smooth as a billiard ball, not a bead of moisture standing on his skin. He nodded and leaned in close. "All right, man: what've you got?"

Time was tight, so the tough ones were asked first. It had been a tricky season for Judge — he led the team in homers and RBIs, but his numbers were down sharply from his rookie year, while his whiff rate was through the roof. He was probed about the strikeouts: Were they the cost of doing business, or did he hope to grow into Albert Pujols, a slugger who walked more often than he whiffed? Judge said that, as a kid, he'd studied Pujols and marvelled at his strict plate discipline. But now, as a professional hitter himself, he couldn't afford to worry about the Ks. "An out is an out, in my opinion. The minute I start thinking about them, I strike out more." Judge's concern was rather with what *led* to the strikeouts: the "curveball he [the pitcher] hangs for me and I don't swing at and now I'm down 0-1. If I don't miss that pitch, I'm standing on second and getting things moving for my teammates."

What did perplex him were his subpar stats and the fact that he hadn't got going for a prolonged stretch. "I feel like I've been grinding since spring training started, playing catch-up with everyone else," he said. He'd had surgery on his shoulder the previous fall and hadn't been able to swing the bat for months. "I've been a little behind, just *trying* to find that hot streak, *trying* to find that hot streak . . ." The stress on the word "trying" said more than its repetition: he was searching for himself in each at-bat. This was three days before the All-Star break, when most of his teammates would scatter to beaches the second their series ended that Sunday. (Stanton, for example, was at a table with models in South Beach *very* early Monday morning.) For Judge, who was starting in left for the AL, there would be no fun in the sun. He'd be haunting the batting cage before and after the game, simulating late-and-close spots. "First and third, one out, bases loaded; two outs, runner on second. Big situation, need a big hit. That's what I live for, do all this extra stuff — I've always loved being in that position."

Which led to the next question: leadership. It is rare, if not unheard of, for a second-year player to declare his authority in the clubhouse. Even if he's ready for it, his teammates aren't: there's a traditional pace and protocol to observe. But in Judge's case, no: on this very young team, his voice carries beyond its years. "I want to lead by example, but I also want the best out of my teammates," he said. "If I see something, I'm going to say it, but not on the field, when emotions are full." Later, on the flight home, when everyone else is sleeping, "I'll say, 'Hey, what happened in the sixth, maybe we should handle it this way,' or, 'I saw what happened after the strikeout. That ain't the right time to be doing that.'"

It was abundantly clear that he was talking about Torres, the kid he'd been mentoring in the shadows. Judge, who was drafted in 2013, spent several spring camps around old-guard leaders like A-Rod and CC Sabathia. The former, for all his defects, was a tough-love tutor for kids like Cano and Melky Cabrera. He pulled them aside and taught them what a work ethic looked like — how to stretch and lift and get your swings in, while staying out of the clubs before a big series. As for CC, Judge couldn't sing his praises enough; Sabathia's was precisely the sort of strength he hoped to model. "After I was drafted, I got to take BP with the team in Oakland," Judge recalled. "CC was starting for us that day, but he called out to me in the lunchroom, 'Hey, Aaron, man, how ya doin', sit over here.' He's probably thinking, 'This kid's never going to play with me,' but he went out of his way to welcome me and see how I was doing." CC's warmth extended to everyone that day: "Whether you had ten years in or you were just called up, he's gonna show you respect," Judge marveled. "The way he treats people is amazing."

Judge could have been talking about himself; the Yanks rave about his tossed-off kindness. There was that moment between innings in Philadelphia when a child in the stands threw a ball to him. Judge caught it at the ankles, looked behind him to check the coast, and proceeded to play catch with the kid. Before batting practice in Baltimore, we saw him approach a kid whose father had driven him hundreds of miles to the game. Judge asked him how his school year was going, but the boy was dumbstruck by nerves. Instinctively, Judge handed him the bat he was carrying. "How's that feel? Kinda heavy, right?" Blushing, the boy half-swung the thirty-four-ouncer and said it felt just right. "I'm glad," said Judge. "It's yours, my guy. Take care of it now for me, huh?"

It would have been nice to ask him where that well of sweetness sprang from, but the allotted time for the sit-down was over. With Judge, half an hour means half an hour. But before getting up, he ventured something revealing. He said that all his life he'd been stared at by people, and that "those weird looks" had prepared him for New York. "You can't go anywhere in this city without people saying something, and being different got me ready for that. Now it's just nothing to me. I say, 'Hey, what's going on?' instead of 'You guys got a problem or something?'"

Hearing that, we harked to another too-tall import: the detestable Big Unit, Randy Johnson. Before his introductory presser to New York in 2005, Johnson barked at a guy who'd pointed a news camera at him. "Don't get in my face, and don't talk back to me!" he snapped at the Channel 2 lensman, Vinny Everett. Johnson, a Yankee for all of ten seconds, had somehow captured the essence of that team before he'd been fitted for a jersey. George's brutes pushed around the little guy, be it the Tampa Bay Rays or that poor sod doing his job. If you weren't opening your wallet, you were in the way, blocking their trip to the bank. These Yanks of Hal Steinbrenner's don't assault strangers; instead, they commit acts of grace. If you want to mark the difference between the reigns of George and Hal, just watch that twenty-second clip of Judge soft-tossing a ball to a ten-year-old boy in the bleachers.

5

CC AND THE (CHIN) MUSIC FACTORY

I f you're driving to Aaron Boone's house in southern Connecticut, Siri will *not* send you the shortest route from his office at Yankee Stadium. That would be Interstate 95-North (or its service road), known to truckers and troopers as the Highway to Hell.

Avoiding the traffic torture at exit 4, your phone will direct you to Rye Brook, New York, snaking you through the woods of Westchester County till you're safely across state lines. Approaching Boone's hamlet, you will find that nature's still in charge here. Big, earth-toned Tudors are snugged into the landscape, discreetly peeking out from foliage. Reception gets patchy as you hunt for his mailbox; stands of plane trees are blocking your meager signal. Finally, you spot it, but the game's still afoot: his house is down a path so bendy and long, it could use its own GPS tag. Negotiating the turns, you arrive in his driveway, where Boone's already stationed at the wheel of his 2018 Mercedes S 560. Shades on, collar up, his hands at two and six, he asks, "You ready?"

Though it's six hours till game time, Boone will be damned if he lets his coaches beat him to the park. Moreover, the way *he* drives, he needs an early start. His tank of a sedan has 463 horses, but Boone never goes above 55 miles per hour, purring over the potholes on the Hutch. The ride is so plush, it's frankly sedating, as if smooth jazz had a baby with

German engineering. To further narcotize you, Boone dials up The Bridge, the Sirius channel that's like a vegetative coma set to seventies pop. Poco, Jim Croce, Pure Prairie League — there isn't a viable sperm cell within a hundred yards of any car tuned to this schmaltz.

But he's been gracious enough to give Klapisch some time alone, away from the din and the madding crowd, so, as much as it must pain him, he turns down the volume to a muzzy rumor. For the next sixty minutes, Boone is peppered with questions about the Red Sox, Joe Torre, and his job specs. But the truth is, no grilling can crack Boone's cone of Zen. Like the shocks on his car and the soundtrack in its cabin, Boone is a tension diffuser. You'll never hear a power riff from *this* guy.

He's spent the morning as he spends all mornings that don't precede a day game in the Bronx: padding around the house after his pretty wife, Laura, and their four young children (two adopted). Laura moved the brood here after their school year ended, and the family's still un-packing, or she is: the kids are busy FaceTiming their friends back in Arizona. So it goes for the progeny of big leaguers. Boone moved six times while he was a player. His current job feels like an anchor, though: the Yanks are out of the business of short-term fixes. Torre and Girardi each lasted a decade; it'd be an upset if Boone didn't surpass them. His bulletproof calm is exactly what Cashman ordered after the grit-jawed grimness of Joe Girardi. Girardi seemed to seek out things to stress him; Boone won't give them the time of day. He doesn't read the papers, doesn't listen to talk radio, and doesn't name-check himself on Twitter. "'Don't read *anything*,' Torre told me when I got to New York," he says. "I've taken his advice."

No one should mistake Boone for Torre 2.0, though you *really* have to see his impression of Joe: he's got that plodding, hands-in-pockets duckwalk down to a fare-thee-well. (Ditto his take on A-Rod in the box: the pursed pillow lips and the faraway gaze as he searches the stands for admirers. Priceless!)

Once parked at his desk before a game, Boone spends hours reading situational data, then files it where he needs it — in his head. Everyone, from Cashman to the clubhouse kids, marvels at Boone's photographic recall. Before the Yankees hired him, they had him take a test in which he was asked to make a lineup using only metrics. Poring over readouts of abstruse numbers — line-drive percentage, contact ratio, batting average on balls put in play — but no player names or lifetime stats, Boone assembled an order that was nearly identical to one the Yanks used in 2018. "It was pretty amazing," says Mike Fishman, their chief of analytics. "By far the best score of the guys we tested."

Jessica Mendoza, Boone's partner in the booth during his *Sunday Night Baseball* stint with ESPN, laughed when she was asked about his work prep. She remembers blowout games that dragged and dragged, but there Boone was in the top of the eighth, breaking down strategy for both pens. "I'd give him crap about it, like, 'Boonie, it's 8–1, no one cares!'" she says. "It was our job to entertain people, not to win games," but Boone remained fixed on player matchups. Cashman saw that doggedness in Boone during his six-hour interview with the Yanks. Over the course of those breakout meetings, they threw the works at him, testing his endurance and processing speed. You can do all the pregame cribbing in the world, but it's useless if your brain's a beat behind. (To that end, Klapisch was having lunch with Davey Johnson, who managed those bawdy Mets teams of the eighties. Johnson scanned his menu and promptly set it down, then watched Klapisch dither over his choices. "Christ, you'd never last a day as a manager. You can't even decide what to *eat*," he snorted.)

Before the car ride with Boone, Klapisch called Don Mattingly. "Donnie Baseball" is another guy who got a skipper's job without any prior coaching experience. Like most players and fans, he thought he could manage a team — until he had to helm an actual game. "If you're not paying attention and making moves without thinking ahead,

I guarantee you'll run out of players," he said. "That's the one thing I learned right away — those little decisions are big later on." Cashman couldn't have known how Boone would respond in late-and-close spots like that, but everything about him tested so high that the decision rendered itself. "We know you can get fooled in interviews, but we have a process designed to give the true result," Cashman notes. "Everything we felt coming out of that room was, *This is unanimous.* And I can tell you right now: we *weren't* fooled. He's backed it up as real."

There was another quality that rang with Cashman in his final assessment of Boone. He clearly, and unreservedly, *cares* for people; he radiates kindness that can't be faked. Mendoza gets emotional when speaking of Boone, who backed her to the hilt during a rough stretch. A former US Olympic softball player, she was the first female analyst hired for national baseball broadcasts. The response to her on Twitter was . . . pre-caveman. "It's the nature of the sport — things that're out of the ordinary are seen as negative," she says. "People told him, 'I can't believe you work with a *woman*.' I'm sure he even heard it from his family. But Aaron would cut them off with, 'It's going to be fine.' He was like a brother to me."

In that eyeblink way he has of reading people, Boone sensed when she'd been checking her online feed. He'd tell her, in his best spa Muzak tone, to stop stressing about being a woman and "just talk baseball." If that didn't work, he'd stage a little gag for her right before they went on air. As the producer counted down, he'd put his hands over his face and shriek, "Oh, my God, *I'm freaking out!*" "The only one freaking out was *me*," says Mendoza. "But he totally made me laugh and calmed me down."

There are people in the world whose aura of peace is a poorly drawn disguise — the handsy yoga instructor; the huckster homeopath; the clerk at the post office whose pace is *soooo* slow. Few of those folks actually have the serenity they espouse — and fewer still inspire it in other people. But that is Boone's gift: to be tranquil but alert, and to project that mind-set onto his players.

During the long car ride, he keeps using the word "culture" to describe the dialectic of his clubhouse. It's hard to get him to pin down what he means, but it's probably some combination of these qualities he keeps citing: the good-guy leadership of Sabathia and Gardner; the team-first selflessness of Judge and Didi; the perfectionist tradecraft of Stanton and Chapman; and the energy of the kids. Most of those players' virtues are hardwired, but Boone gives them the stage for full expression. That very first meeting with the players in Tampa, Boone let them know that he planned to have a ball and that they should expect to as well. *You do your work before the games, you study the data we provide you, and this year's gonna be GREAT.* Puzzled, the players glanced at each other, expecting a shoe to drop. But no, that was it. Class dismissed.

Under Girardi, the players scurried hither and yon like they were bustling between classes in high school. Joe scheduled every minute of every day and posted the timeline on a whiteboard. Boone does precisely none of that stuff — he delegates those duties to his lieutenants. Marcus Thames, the hitting coach, runs the offense; Larry Rothschild handles the pitching. *They* run the position meetings before each game, while Boone's in his office or out on the field, watching and shouting encouragement during drills.

One day in the summer, he was seen standing in the outfield, kibitzing with Gary Sánchez. Sánchez, the closest thing to a coach-killer on the team, was in the thick of rehab for his groin. (He'd landed on the DL in late June.) Barred from jogging, he was keeping his arm limber, having a long toss with one of the coaches. It was bracing to hear the sharp *thwack!* of Sánchez's throws as they hit the glove a hundred feet away. Boone, in his hoodie, grinned like a pre-teen looking on. He was giddily getting off on Sánchez's arm strength and having himself a hoot at three o'clock. But he was also sending a message to his mood-challenged catcher: *I'm here for you, man. I care. We're in this together.*

A month or so later, Sánchez would test Boone's faith. In an ugly game in Tampa, Sánchez disgraced himself with two acts of insurrection. In the first inning, he handed the Rays a cheap run by not scurrying after a passed ball. In the ninth, he jogged out a grounder to short with a man on first — and was beaten by the *relay* throw from the second baseman to first and thus made the last out of the game. The Yanks lost by a run, fell another game behind the surging Red Sox, and were quietly furious at their teammate. He had a history of this kind of stuff, going all the way back to A-ball, where he was suspended for a blatant lack of hustle. No one knew why Sánchez did it, and Sánchez wasn't saying. After the game, he simply said: "I'm sorry."

The Twitterverse lost its mind. Everywhere you turned, there were calls for his head, beginning with a stiff suspension. Beneath the outrage, an undercurrent was heard: *Let's see how that softy Boone handles THIS.* But Boone kept the pitchfork types waiting a night — he said he wanted to watch the videotape. The next day the Yankees punted the matter, returning Sánchez to the DL with a groin strain. But Boone still had to face the press before the next game with the Rays. Swarmed in the visitors' dugout, he stuck to his guns — which, in his case, meant keeping them holstered. While allowing that his catcher had "to do better," he refused to throw Sánchez to the dogs. "I believe in the player," he said several times, sounding like a priest standing up for a kid who'd snuck out of Mass to boost a Yoo-hoo. In a firm but even tone, Boone was making it clear that he'd run this team as he saw fit — and that he wouldn't be doing so through the press. In this era, you only get to keep your job if you win *and* know how to guard your players.

And that, essentially, was that. Writers groused in their columns about the "convenience" of Sánchez's groin injury, then moved on to something else the following day. The incident wasn't forgotten — nothing is in New York — and would be revived when Sánchez jaked it in the future. But Boone had flipped the script from indictment to affirmation and proved himself a uniter, not a divider. That's the sort of statement that rings in a clubhouse, not just during the season but beyond it.

This point is raised because it underscores a truth: baseball has changed a lot, but its core audience hasn't. In their heart of hearts, the sport's lunch-pail fans yearn for the bullies who ruled by fear. They miss Big Stein and his back-page fist-shakes at stars who underperformed when it counted. (See Dave "Mr. May" Winfield, for one example.) The sports-chat talkers respected Girardi because they thought he was feared and not liked. When pushed by a player, he pushed back harder, putting Sánchez on blast for all to hear. Girardi's only flaw, in their eyes, was not being Billy Martin, the wild man who went at Reggie Jackson during a game and punched his pitcher, Ed Whitson, in a bar fight.

Sports have *always* been a proxy for something else, but these days baseball feels like a fight between its past and present. Which is precisely what makes a manager like Boone so interesting. He refuses to play by the tough-guy dictums handed down by men before him. Even if he wanted to, he knows it wouldn't work; these ballplaying millennials wouldn't stand for it. "If George were still alive, he'd be sued out of baseball," a Yankees executive observed last spring. "The players these days would have him in court so fast, he'd be *glad* for a suspension" (from the commissioner).

Torre survived being soft on players by strenuously seducing the press. (And by winning four titles.) He entertained reporters for a half-hour before games, packing them into the dugout to hear his tales of Bob Gibson till everyone recited them under their breath. But there were methods to Joe's nostalgizing madness. By gobbling up their time during batting practice, he kept writers from wandering into the clubhouse and getting something good from one of his players. More, he earned credit with most of the beat writers, who were deluded into thinking he liked them. Boone, by contrast, won't fraternize with writers. He's never less than genial, but he doesn't have them into his office or gossip off the record about his boss. The writers seem to like him and are willing to live without the access they had in the Torre years. Affections in this town run thin, however. You had to wonder how the press would treat him if his Yankees punched out early in October.

There's one other thing about Boone worth discussing, in part because Boone himself won't: that day he went in for open-heart surgery in March 2009. Boone was born with a congenital defect called bicuspid aortic valve disease (BAVD); it occurs in about 2 percent of live births. Most aortic valves have three flaps, or leaflets, that meter the flow of blood from heart to aorta. Boone has only two, a condition that can lead to clots (and early death) as the valve calcifies. Patients with BAVD typically reach middle age before they need surgical intervention; Boone was among the few whose valve deteriorated in his middle thirties. At the time, he was near the end of his playing days, a good but not great career spent at third base. (His brother Bret, a three-time All-Star, made the bigger dent playing second.) In a routine physical before spring training with the Astros, Boone was stunned to learn that his heart condition had worsened: he needed surgery — soon — to resection the valve.

He checked himself into the Stanford Medical Center in Palo Alto, California. All his storied clan, and several close friends, flew in to lend support. Bret sat on his brother's bed the morning of the operation and asked the surgeon, Dr. Craig Miller, what the risks were. Miller told him not to worry, he'd done the procedure hundreds of times. But the Boone brothers *were* worried: it was an eight-hour ordeal in which Aaron's chest would be sawed and cracked open. "Aaron was really scared; it was a humbling time for him," Bret said. "He'd always been a faithful, churchgoing guy, but the operation took it to another level." The night before he went under, Boone wrote letters to his wife and kids. "We'd just had Brandon, and my daughter Bella hadn't been born yet. If something happened to me, I wanted them to have those," he told Klapisch. He entrusted the letters to his friend Ryan Stromsborg, with an injunction ("just in case"), and said no more.

He'd always been known as a sweetheart in the game: relaxed, convivial, popular around the clubhouse. (Bret calls him "the likable Boone.") But after the operation — a complete success — his mood went black for a time. "He was depressed and snappy, a very different guy," says Laura, who was caught unawares. They'd prepped themselves beforehand as best they could — met "a ton of people who'd had the operation, including families whose kids went through it," she adds — but were blindsided by its aftermath. The thing she'd prized most in him — that he's "built to stand high pressure" — was tested in full that spring. Eventually, the cloud lifted and Boone was back to being himself, only more so in ways that are hard to name. "The people who reached out to me after the fact — frankly, it was overwhelming," he says. That "outpouring of care and love" made him appreciative, says his brother. After he recovered, "he was a better husband and dad." Laura, it bears saying, wound up with her husband's letters. She kept them, but never opened and read them. No interest, she says now. "They're too eerie."

Boone, as mentioned, is terse about the surgery, but agrees that it reset his sense of scale. Time was, he was a guy who sweated his stats and drove himself crazy during slumps. "I had *been* that hitter who goes to the park thinking, *I need to get a hit tonight*," he tells us. All that worrying did was to freeze him in the box and make a short swoon last longer. "That's how the game'll knock you to your knees. There has to be a balance: pour yourself into your prep, then go up to the plate and say, 'Screw it.'"

He's responding to queries about the Red Sox, who, at that point in the season, lead the Yanks by five games. Boston came out of the gates on fire, playing .700 ball in April and keeping up that pace, or close to it, through July. At the All-Star break, they'd put up numbers like nothing in their 118-year span. They had the most wins in history before the All-Star Game (68); were on pace to win 112 games, seven more than their best mark ever; fielded the leaders in every hitting stat that mattered; and started four pitchers with ten or more wins for the first time since Baltimore did it in '77. Nailbiters or blowouts, day games or night — all they ever seem to do is win.

This feels, in the scheme of things, grossly unfair, especially to Yankees fans. The Yanks are having their own smash season — winning the second-most games in baseball, threatening the season record for home runs, and redefining excellence out of the pen — but they find themselves hanging off the Red Sox rudder like Tom Cruise shooting a stunt. No matter that they've pitched superbly and weathered injuries; Boston is simply better across the board. The Red Sox hit a ton of homers but don't rely on them; they lead the league in runs and total bases. They are splendid at Fenway and brilliant away. In fact, their home and road splits are almost a match. And unlike the Yankees, the Sox are ruthlessly efficient when playing in their division. On July 31 — the day of the trade deadline — Boston stood 29-9 against Baltimore, Tampa, and Toronto. The Yanks were 20-15. Small wonder they keep losing ground to the Sox. They haven't handled their business in the AL East.

But when this issue is raised in the car with Boone, he doesn't bat an eye. Despite attempts to engage him about the Sox, and the difficulty of managing against a rival that seems to do everything right, Boone keeps circling back to his players, saying that they are his only focus. Even asking about the crapshoot of playing a wild-card game fails to get a rise from him. "I mean, what good does worrying do for anyone?" he says. "Of course I like it when the Red Sox lose, but either we're good enough or we aren't. If all you're gonna do is worry about results, you'll just play tight and lose." From day one in Tampa, his doctrine to the players has been: Let the competition decide. Consume every metric, sharpen your mechanics, and take care of your body between starts. But once you've done those things . . . screw it, play the game. *Let the competition decide.*

As if to test his dictate, brake lights loom ahead: traffic suddenly bunches up on the Deegan. Boone checks his navigation: there are stop-and-go delays to the exit for 95. He gives a semi-shrug and settles in his seat. It's more than five hours till first pitch. Apparently, once a man's had his chest wall split open, some light bumper-to-bumper doesn't churn his heart.

There are — or so we've heard — three phases of a man's pride. In phase one, he's the teen who won't keep his shirt on, doffing it at the park (or the dinner table) to share his peach-fuzzed six-pack with the world. In phase two, he's got dad-flab and won't take his shirt *off*, aghast at what's become of himself since college. In phase three, our balding geezer has given up caring and parades around the house in shirtless glory, patting his paunch in contentment. Generally, phase-three man is either past or approaching sixty and free of the things that once perturbed him. Sex and parenting and blunted ambition — all those worries are well behind him. What lies ahead now are the many comforts of the fridge and a free hand with the remote.

Unless, of course, the man is CC Sabathia, a great grizzly of a guy who's found a second prime at the age of thirty-eight. To watch him in the clubhouse sans shirt, grinning as he lugs around that three-roll mass, is to see a man so comfortable in his skin, you'd think he got a back rub from Buddha. Every day is a gift now, a karmic reward for the kindness he's shown others in his career. It's also an affirmation of who he's become: the wise old monk who had a crisis of the soul and came through it renewed and secure. During the car ride, Boone praises CC as the keeper of "our culture," a leader whose jollity sets the tone in the room and whose steadiness keeps it on course. In temperament, Boone and CC are like psychic twins: optimists at peace with where life has brought them and protectors of that precious thing called *team*. With some help from Judge and Didi, they've spun a tight structural web that can take the wind and rain.

Sabathia, a warhorse of eighteen seasons in the bigs, is surprised and delighted to still be here. "Yeah, I'm old!" he exclaimed, with a raucous laugh, when told that he could be Gleyber Torres's dad. "But I'm having more fun now than when I was young. It's a great team to [play on]. I'm just — *happy*." He knows it could go away at any second; his health is pitch to pitch, not week to week. "Some days, if I've had a bad game, I'm like, 'That's it, I'm going home!'" he said, sitting at his locker. "But when I'm throwing the ball well, it's like, 'I could do this for five years.' It all depends how my health holds up."

He has bone-on-bone arthritis in his right, or landing, knee, and he's facing joint replacement when he retires. He must also win nightly stare-downs with the minibar, at least when the Yanks are on the road. This is his third season of sobriety. Oh, and it's been years since he lost the hair on his splendid four-seam fastball. Time was, from 2001 till the 2012 season, Sabathia would rock back, pause his high-kick windup, and blow 97 by you up and in. Beating a hitter who's sitting on hard stuff is like dunking over LeBron: a pitcher's primal scream of brute dominion. All the great ones did it until they didn't, and very few had the verve to win without it. Warren Spahn, Bob Feller, Tom Seaver, Pedro Martínez — only a select group had the wit and want-to to reinvent themselves at thirty-five. All of those men are in the Hall of Fame. Sabathia, if there's any justice, will join them there.

As beloved as Judge is on the streets of New York, he runs second to Sabathia in the clubhouse. Among pitchers and the kids who've joined the team these last two years, Sabathia is the teddy bear at the back of the room, a merry combination of Cliff Huxtable and Dr. Phil, with some Cedric the Entertainer tossed in. Before every home game, he holds a raucous chat with four or five guys grouped around him — Betances and Severino, Sonny Gray and Jordan Montgomery (who spent more of the year on the disabled list), plus one or two of the arms on the Scranton shuttle. They might be yakking about LeBron as an LA Laker or the Eagles' chances of repeating in the NFC, but what's actually going on there is a therapy session disguised as front-porch patter. Everyone's laughing and talking past each other and getting the last word in — and none of them are worrying about their lousy outing the night or two before.

Sabathia's prime beneficiaries are Betances and Sonny Gray — Betances because he sometimes loses his release point and melts down on the mound, and Gray because he's wound up like a top and needs to breathe out for half an hour. You can see it in his posture when he sits with CC. As his shoulders soften and his jaw unclamps, he looks about five years younger. That gift that Sabathia has for putting people at ease — you can't overpraise its value to a team living under the gun. Each night the Yankees glance at the scoreboard in center and see the Red Sox winning . . . *again*. It's both surreal and depleting, like a run-on dream of sprinting while your feet are tied together.

When Sabathia arrived in 2009, he was no one's idea of a guru. He was a sweet but reticent giant who seemed plainly relieved to play fifth fiddle on a team. "Jeter and A-Rod and Posada and Andy — all I was trying to do was fit in," he tells us. "It was easier being a Yankee than an Indian or Brewer because I didn't have to carry that team. It made life a whole lot simpler."

For four years, Sabathia was the Big Dependable. He won eighteen or nineteen games a season, pitched to an ERA in the low threes, and struck out a couple of hundred hitters. He'd been blessed with the setup to throw hard for eight innings: an industrial set of shoulders, tractor-pull quads, and huge and rubbery hips. What you missed in all that mass was his pure athleticism — the agility to bring his knee to his chest and keep his weight centered over the slab as he launched off his plant leg to throw. Years ago, Dwight Gooden talked about his own windup, which was the most glorious motion in sports in the 1980s. A hundred times a game, he'd corkscrew at the waist, raise his left knee till it almost grazed his chin, then plow through to finish over that knee. But come the nineties, he could barely lift the foot to his waist — and even that was hell for five innings. "That's where you lose the power, when your legs are stiff and you can't finish off pitches," Doc observed.

It was worse for Sabathia, who was transferring all that torque to a joint ground down by attrition. Though he didn't tell anyone about the pain, it loused up his follow-through. His stride got shorter as he favored the knee, taking miles and revolutions off his heater. Suddenly, he threw 92, not 97, leaving it up in the zone. That's a recipe for a beating, and Sabathia caught one, trying to grit through with off-speed stuff. By the summer of '13, the guy who took pride in going deep into games couldn't get out of the sixth inning. Opposing hitters crushed him in his third turn through the order, batting .370 against him through season's end. As bad as getting kicked around by Boston was, worse was being pressed by the tabloid guys to explain his plodding fastball. He'd always stood tall at his locker after games, talking till the last guy left. Now he got surly and scarce. When he wasn't in the trainer's room, he gave clipped answers and resented the writers who asked the questions.

That season — 2013 — was hell for everyone. Teixeira hurt his wrist at the World Baseball Classic and spent most of the year healing, or trying to. Curtis Granderson was plunked twice and missed 101 games with a fractured forearm and finger. Alex Rodríguez was popped for steroids by the commissioner's office, but got the suspension stayed for a year. All summer, reporters camped out at his locker. It was like covering Reggie back in the day. You had to be there just in case another land mine went off.

A-Rod's ban the following year and the signing of B-plus stars (Ellsbury, Beltrán, McCann) did nothing to improve the mood. Jeter's farewell tour and its ceaseless coverage in the press sucked the air from the room. It seemed as though the Yankees were stuck in the doldrums. Sabathia, mired in his own despond, couldn't help with morale that season. The pain in his knee was so bad that he stopped pitching in May and spent the rest of the season in grueling rehab. He'd been told that he would need a joint replacement, and the stopgap measure — repeat injections of Orthovisc, a synthetic goo that mimics cartilage — wasn't taking. Up against the end of a grand career, Sabathia numbed his sorrows with booze. He didn't drink in public or show up to the park reeking, but something was clearly wrong with him. You could see it in his bearing, a kind of dull fatigue that tracked him on the field and off.

By the 2015 season, word got around that CC's boozing had spiked after road games. He'd hole up in his suite, where no one could see him, and wipe out the stock in his mini-fridge. That August he was filmed outside a bar in Toronto, gesturing and yelling taunts at a patron. As blows began to fly, someone stuffed him into a sedan, missing one of his shoes. Six weeks later, he checked into a clinic at the urging of his wife. Sabathia broke the news on the last day of the season. He was somewhere in treatment when the Yanks played the Astros in a wildcard game at the Stadium. His absence italicized the Yanks' shutout loss. Sabathia and his team had bottomed out.

All of which made for a certain symmetry: as Sabathia went, so went the Yankees. Since he signed in '09, his movements and the team's had closely mirrored each other, beginning with their triumph that title season. Over the next three years, CC and the team would both have fine regular seasons and hard-to-figure pratfalls in October. Ditto the dark years of 2013–2015, when everything went south at once: injuries, scandals, old age having its way. This pattern made their joint resurrection in 2016 all the more stunning to behold. Sabathia came to camp that spring humbled and clear-eyed after his treatment in rehab. He spoke candidly to the press about losing his way when his body began to break down. "I was tired of being in the dark about [my drinking]," he told the *News*. "I had dealt with it from the end of 2012 to that point. It was more exhausting than actually drinking — trying to hide [it]."

CC's fastball was gone, but he'd come to terms with that too and was committed to pitching without it. He'd found an expensive knee brace that stabilized the joint and kept the bones from rubbing against each other. It wasn't a perfect fix: the thing was huge and clumsy, making it hard to field his position. If you laid one down on him, you'd have yourself a hit — and a pitch between your ears in your next at-bat.

But the other work-around, the cutter taught him by Andy Pettitte? *That* was an unqualified triumph. There are essentially three fastballs that pitchers use these days. The most common, the four-seamer, travels straight and true and is the one thrown at peak velocity. The two-seamer tails and dips at the plate, acting like a harder changeup; Max Scherzer has the best one on the planet. And the cutter, as perfected by Mo Rivera, breaks late and hard on lefty hitters, sawing the bat off in their hands. What Sabathia was pleased to learn was that his cutter and two-seamer look *exactly alike* to hitters. They come in at virtually the same speed — 90.2 miles per hour for the two-seamer, 88.9 for the cutter — but veer in opposite ways that last split second. Better still, he can throw them with a draftsman's precision to either side of the plate.

Instead of swings and misses, he now gets feeble hacks from hitters who've been fooled by the location of his pitch. He can still run his four-seam up there at 93 and generally flashes it a couple times a game. But soft contact leads to shorter at-bats and longer, more productive outings. Since August of '16, when he mastered the cutter, he's averaged six innings a start, has an ERA of 3.46, and has won twice as many games as he's lost. Over that span, only a handful of pitchers have been better at producing soft outs. None of them, safe to say, have pitched on one knee or done more with less arm speed than CC Sabathia.

It's funny how these things work in baseball. Back in '15, when Sabathia had an ERA in the high fours and a salary of $24 million, the Yankees couldn't wait for him to quit. All their restless talk of "getting under the luxury tax" was a memo to CC and A-Rod: *Retire!* The money they'd save when those two left could be spent on a pair of fresh horses. They'd have a choice card to pick from if they bided their time: José Fernández, Matt Harvey, and Clayton Kershaw would be free agents in the golden class of '19. Fernández, the marvel who'd made two All-Star Games before he turned twenty-four, would almost surely have leapt at a Yankee offer. He and Stanton, good friends and teammates in Miami, talked openly about going to the Bronx when they hit the free-agent market. But one night near the end of the '16 season, Fernández got high and drunk on his boat and plowed it into a jetty at fifty knots. He and two of his buddies were killed on impact. In June of that season, Harvey's arm gave out for the second time in four years. (He returned the following season a ghost of himself, shredded by overuse and New York's nightlife. He eventually got dealt to the Cincinnati Reds for Devin Mesoraco.) The same month Harvey went down, Kershaw came up lame. The three-time Cy Young winner threw a disc and would miss chunks of the next three seasons with a back condition and lose four or five miles off his fastball.

In short, none of those stallions proved as sturdy — or bankable — as the old doughy guy in the knee brace. When Sabathia's deal vested for an option for 2017, per the terms of the extension he signed in 2011, the Yankees gladly re-upped him in '18. At $10 million, Sabathia was a steal, the rare case of Cashman getting off cheap.

In 2017, Sabathia was 10-0 in starts after Yankees losses. More importantly, he was 4-0 against *Boston,* the team pitchers are judged by in the Bronx. It was more of the same for most of '18: he went undefeated against winning teams and posted his biggest wins after Yankee losses. That's how you avoid the kind of slide that can cost you a division title. In 2018, the Yanks were the last team in baseball to drop three games in a row; meanwhile, they ran off seven streaks of three or more wins. Homers aside, it wasn't entirely clear how they kept on winning. None of their franchise hitters were having great years, and one of their most dangerous hitters, Sánchez, was batting .190. Their starters were slightly better than projected — with the exception of Gray, who was dreadful — and their fielding stats were middle-of-the-pack, hurt by rookie gaffes from Torres and Andújar. It was mostly resilience — a miscellaneous toughness — that kept the Yanks within striking distance of the Sox. No one better embodied that grit than Sabathia. Start after start, he'd go out there throwing soft-serve and hand a lead or a close game to the pen. At bargain wages, he was what Tanaka and Severino weren't: a certifiable stopper. He nipped slumps before they had a chance to happen and gave the Yanks a chance each time he pitched.

Of course, it's never a stellar sign when a team's most trusted starter is a gimpy vet closing in on forty. For all of New York's wins, there were cracks in the foundation, a gnawing sense that the center might not hold. In too many games, the Yanks failed at small-ball basics — moving a runner along, getting a bunt down when it mattered — while waiting on three-run shots to bust it open. They struck out far too often for a team chasing a title; in the AL, only Texas and the White Sox were whiffing at a greater rate. And the bullpen, while mostly brilliant, was beginning to tire, since the starters rarely gave them seven innings.

Every team has holes, even the very best ones. The Red Sox lacked relievers to hand leads to Craig Kimbrel. The Astros needed a closer and at least another bat, after passing on J. D. Martinez in the winter. But *those* clubs weren't five games out and burning through their gas to keep up. Cashman wasn't available to check his gauges; he and his staff were hunkered down till the trading deadline. But weeks before the deadline at the end of July, pressure mounted on him to make an impact deal. His team was short a starter capable of going deep into games and proving he could beat the Sox, a rental catcher who could sub for the ailing Sánchez, and a guy to spell Judge a day or two in right while hitting *something* besides homers off the bench.

Meanwhile — inevitably — the Yanks began to stall. They'd lost Sánchez the first time on June 24, and a month later he'd return to the DL. (In total, he'd miss two months of the season.) Torres strained a hip in early July and missed three weeks around the All-Star break. Then Severino, the Cy Young leader through June, suddenly hit the skids and stopped winning. He couldn't command his fastball, which stayed up in the zone. It got smoked, early and often, for loud hits. In his first nineteen starts, batters hit .214 against his high-test heater. Over the next four, they hit .397. But something else was off: Severino was tipping pitches. As *Sports Illustrated*'s Tom Verducci was the first to note, Severino had a tell when he pitched from a windup. He raised his left heel higher to throw a slider than a fastball, flushing the value of his second-best pitch. He didn't have much of a changeup, so hitters sat on his hard stuff when he pitched with the bases empty. For five innings, they'd pound him and fatten his pitch count, then finish him off in the sixth.

As their stars faltered, so did the Yanks: they played .500 ball for an entire month. The team was on fumes by the All-Star break, and no one needed the reset more than Judge. He'd gotten only two games off the entire season and looked frankly gassed. Beginning in June, when he hit .234, his drives stopped carrying out of the park. He was asked if his shoulder was acting up. He said no, he was just missing good pitches. In any case, a break was what he needed. He skipped the Home Run Derby, hit a dinger in the AL's 8–6 win, and came out of the gate in the second half with a pair of three-hit games and his first homer that counted in three weeks.

Then, on July 26, in a home game against the Royals, Judge was clipped by a pitch. The high heat from Jakob Junis barely missed his jaw, catching him on the heel of his right hand. The crowd at the Stadium went stone silent. Judge managed to take his base, then left the game soon after. X-rays showed a fracture at the top of his wrist; that ulnar styloid chip would cost him almost two months.

The news could have been much, much worse, of course: he'd narrowly dodged a beaning and months of rehab. But the *timing* of the injury was bad indeed — the Yanks were gearing up for a series in Fenway that would probably tell the tale. Yes, they'd still have fifty games to play, but that four-game set in Boston now loomed as make-or-break. If they won three of four, they'd chop the lead to three and declare that they were in this till the end. Conversely, losing three (or more) meant waving the flag and resigning themselves to a wild-card berth.

Though no one seemed to notice till after the All-Star break, the A's were gaining fast in the wild-card hunt, and the Mariners, recovered from their beatdown in the Bronx, were running neck and neck with them. A one-game play-in was a bleak enough prospect for a Yankee team on course to win a hundred. Missing a wild card altogether would be a debacle for the ages and would put Cashman and his culture under the lens. He probably wouldn't be the scapegoat, though; that would be his nice-guy rookie skipper. You could almost see the headline write itself: "Beleaguered Boone Blows It Down the Stretch."

Cashman did, of course, summon reinforcements: he made three deals to patch his pitching staff. J. A. Happ, the cerebral lefty, was a front-end starter who seemed to save his best games for the Sox. Lance Lynn and his burly heater were acquired from the Twins; he'd had five terrific seasons in St. Louis before falling on his face in Minnesota. Both men were upgrades over Gray and cost the Yankees little in long-term assets. Zach Britton, the Orioles' closer, came more dearly: Cashman sent three of his B-plus chips in Josh Rogers, Cody Carroll, and Dillon Tate. That trade struck observers as a peculiar one: Cashman was splurging on an area of strength instead of dealing for a need. He also neglected to add a veteran bat, someone like Steve Pearce, whom the Red Sox grabbed. But the questions about his choices would have to wait. Cashman hunkered down until mid-August.

Thus fortified, the Yanks put a nice run together, including their first win streak in weeks. Happ pitched superbly in his Bronx debut, going six strong for his eleventh win. Tanaka beat the Orioles for his seventh in a row, a twelve-start span in which he missed a month but chopped his ERA by two runs. Torres was back and heating up, Andújar had hit his way up to the six-hole, and Stanton quietly became their bedrock player, raising his average fifty points. To be sure, they missed Judge, and they didn't try to soft-pedal it. "Look, Aaron is great: he slugs and gets on base," Boone said. "We're not the same team without him." "The whole dynamic of how pitchers attack us changes with him gone," said Stanton, who was suddenly pitched around in Judge's absence.

They also rued heading to Boston without Sánchez: he *owned* the Sox in that park. He'd posted a .973 OPS up there and hit a homer every ten at-bats. In the absence of two of their stars, though, the Yanks had held the line. Their power numbers were down, but they'd won some close games and climbed back to thirty games over .500. That was their toughness showing, a fuck-you pride that said, *We concede nothing, you bastards.*

They'd march into Fenway with their chests stuck out and send their best soldier to the mound. Sabathia — who else? — was going in game 1.

6

"WE MIGHT BE A LITTLE SHORT THIS YEAR"

The Yankees went to Boston in a vulgar mood, furious at themselves for looking ahead. In the final leg of a critical home stand, they'd turned in a shameful, who-cares showing against the worst team in baseball, the Orioles. Sonny Gray, who'd seemed to save his season with three solid wins in a row, went out and pitched himself off the rotation, getting rocked for seven runs in two-plus innings. It might have been his last start ever in the Bronx, where his ERA was 7.71. If so, he certainly sent up an unexpected salute: he cocked his cap and smirked at the crowd of forty-seven thousand when it booed him to the showers.

To be fair, they should have saved some of that hate for Gray's teammates. Twice, Torres failed to cover a base, and the first of those brain-farts led to a five-run inning. And twice the Yankees flopped with the bases full in a game they'd lose, 7–5. (Neil Walker bounced into a double play, and Stanton struck out swinging.) That ran the team's fail-streak to oh-for-fifteen with the bases loaded and highlighted the lineup's year-long struggles with runners in scoring position (RISP).

For four months, the Yanks ranked last in the majors, hitting .161 with RISP. The Red Sox, who were first, featured three of the clutchest bats in the game—Xander Bogaerts, Andrew Benintendi, and J. D. Martinez. To compound their sins, the Yanks had lost that day to a pitcher who'd struggled all year. Alex Cobb didn't sign till the last week

of March, and it showed in his numbers: he was 2-14 with a six-plus
ERA. But he held the Yanks to a run in six innings before his bullpen
made life interesting in the ninth. Here was another dismal habit of
the Yanks: their hitters saved their worst for brand-Z starters. Joe Bi-
agini (1-6, 6.88 ERA), Andrew Cashner (3-10, 4.83), Kendall Grave-
man (1-5, 7.60), Jakob Junis, the Judge-plunking heel (6-11, 5.00) — the
Yankees lost to them all, and meekly too, scoring four earned runs in
twenty-four innings. That failure to beat up no-name pitchers boded ill
for the opener against the Red Sox. Chris Sale, the seven-time All-Star,
had been scratched from the start with a bout of shoulder soreness.
His replacement was Brian Johnson, a back-of-the-bullpen lefty who'd
— naturally — blanked the Yankees in three appearances.

In the clubhouse before game 1, the Yankees paced like boxers,
beaming bad intentions. Then they went out throwing haymakers at
the Sox and bulled them against the ropes early. Didi, batting third,
hit a three-run rocket before Johnson recorded an out. Hicks blasted
another bomb in the second inning, a solo shot that cleared the pen
in right. Far from exalted, though, the Yanks looked rattled: Sabathia,
their savior, had nothing. He labored mightily in the first, walked a run
home in the second, then fell apart in the third. His cutter leaked over
the heart of the plate, and the two-seamer skewed wild outside. The
Red Sox saw this and spat on the latter, waiting for the cutter down the
middle.

Then, once on base, the Sox acted on something else: Sabathia was
tipping his move to home plate. Afterward, the Sox kept mum on what
they'd spotted. After all, they'd get Sabathia twice again in the regular season. But they ran on him at every chance, showing their elder
no respect. Betts stole easily after leading off the first, and then, after
a Steve Pearce bomb in the third, Martinez, the lead-legged slugger,
swiped second.

Sabathia was both flustered and embarrassed. The bill of his cap poured off perspiration. After Martinez stole, Blake Swihart nubbed a roller to the mound. Sabathia sailed his throw past Greg Bird's head. After three, Boone was forced to pull CC, who'd thrown *seventy-seven* pitches and was flying blind without his cutter and two-seamer.

In came Jonathan Holder, one of the season's sweet surprises. An unknown quantity when the Yanks broke camp, he'd climbed what Cashman calls "the credibility tree" with dozens of no-fuss innings. For three months, he'd expertly mixed his plus fastball with a chin-to-shin changeup. But he'd never pitched at Fenway in a pressure game, and on this night the moment overwhelmed him. The Sox ignored his heater and swung at his change, spraying bullets off the left-field wall. Holder faced seven batters and retired none; all of them would end up scoring. It was misery to watch the poor kid implode, but *more* painful was the way his team responded. Boone stared impassively from the top step of the dugout as Holder took his lumps. Neither he nor Rothschild went out to nurse him through it. So, too, Boone's fielders. They stood at their positions, grooming dirt with their cleats. None of them checked on Holder at the mound.

By the time the carnage had ended, the Yanks were down six runs. They crypt-walked through the next five innings: no anger, no push-back, not even a dust-off pitch after Pearce bashed his third of three homers. After the game, the Yanks sat, stunned, at their lockers, mouthing rote answers to pointed questions. *Have to turn the page. Have to right the ship. We're a better team than what we showed.* Well, yes, they were better than a 15–7 butt-kick, but that was no comfort to all concerned. The Sox had just corroborated what everyone else knew: *they* were the team of the year, and maybe the decade. For months, the Yanks had watched with eyebrows arched as the Sox steamrolled the rest of the sport. *Yep, they're strong,* they'd grunt, but there was always an unsaid *but . . . but they'll never do that to* us. Now, after this beat-down, there was no qualifying clause. Instead, the unsaid thought was:

They're just better. Only Gardner, the salty vet, summoned any outrage. "It might be one loss, but this is tough to forget. We *can't* let it continue tomorrow."

At the postgame dais, Boone was grilled on why he'd left Holder in to take a beating. He could have spoken the truth — *I was trying to save my bullpen. We've got three more games here.* Instead, he tiptoed past the subject, saying, "I hoped he'd find it out there." Boone called the gaffes by his fielders "frustrating," but you heard no thread of outrage in his voice. Instead, he stuck to his Stuart Smalley routine. "I still believe in this team," he said several times. "I know we're really good."

The next night, a Friday, the other penny fell: Boone was punked by Alex Cora, the Red Sox skipper. After Gardner was hit by a pitch leading off the top of the first, Severino buzzed Mookie Betts in the bottom half. Betts fell back as if shot, but wasn't grazed; the umpire gave a warning to both teams. Cora raced out at him, screaming blue murder. The ump tossed him from the game, but Cora wasn't leaving till he got his money's worth: he stood on the top step of the Red Sox dugout, shrieking "*Fuck* you, man! Fuck you!" at the Yankees. The Yanks players looked at Boone. Boone looked at Cora — and never said a word, let alone a fuck-you back. He was caught in the vise of his high-road brand: if he cursed out Cora, he might have saved face but been seen as fake by his team. If he took a run at Cora — as *Girardi* surely would have — he'd have proved a point but betrayed his own ethos. At some point in a season, every manager faces a choice between his dignity and his reputation. Boone made his choice and paid a stiff price. The Yankees went down without a peep in games 2 and 3.

On Sunday, several hours before the capper of the series, Klapisch talked privately with one of the veterans in the Yankees' clubhouse. It was coroner-quiet in the visitors' room, and players dressed like they were sneaking out of a house. Klapisch asked the veteran what the hell had just happened: three games, three debacles, zero fire. The veteran looked around him and then muttered, shockingly, "Looks like we might be a little short this year."

Usually, when a player says such a thing, you arrange to call him later for more details. Except there is no "usual" for such a thing: players on a contender *never* say that. They might tell you the team's banged up and/or battling through a slump, but here was a guy admitting, in early August, that his club was cooked. He said it in confidence, knowing he wouldn't be named and that the quote wouldn't run till the following spring. But he was giving last rites for a season still in progress, and for a team that would welcome back Judge and Sánchez for September and beyond.

There's no point rubbing salt into the wound of game 4, when Chapman gagged in the bottom of the ninth and flushed a three-run cushion. It was the first time all year the Yankees blew a game in which they took a lead into the ninth (they'd been 69-0 to that point), but somehow the 5–4 loss felt fated — or worse, beside the point. More notable by far was the team's response to being swept four games at Fenway. None of the clubhouse leaders said what needed saying: that they'd played like garbage and disgraced themselves but would be ready, come the playoffs, when they saw the Sox again.

In a weekend of stark surprises, this was the most revealing — the Yankees lacked *that* guy to send a message. Klapisch was there when Keith Hernandez ripped his Mets in '86, calling out pitchers who phoned it in and hitters who didn't pull their weight. And Klapisch was there in the 2000s when Jason Giambi stepped up, saying, "We suck now. Better turn this shit around fast." On contenders, *someone* has to be the guy who gets his team's attention, be it calling a players' meeting and speaking from the heart or talking to his teammates, sternly, through the press. Maybe Judge would grow into the role in two or three years, or Cashman would add someone over the winter who had the stones and stature to take it on. For now, though, the Yanks lacked a crucial component: a hard-ass who could pull the team out of a ditch.

When a club has no in-house toughie to lean on, the manager has to fill in where he can. It's not about knocking over a buffet table; those stunts went out with Whitey Herzog. Instead, it's about finding a tone and a theme that cuts through the funk his club is in. But as he left Boston for a set against the White Sox, Boone was trailed by hard questions. Was he merely a nice guy built for sunny days, or was there a side of him his players hadn't seen yet? If he suddenly raised his voice to them, would the players listen? Or would they dismiss it as a stunt and tune him out? Because make no mistake: he'd lost some equity in Boston. Cora had outmanned and outmaneuvered him all series, burning hotter and brighter for his team. It doesn't take an SOB to run a baseball club, but you do need to *be* one now and then. That's all part of the job for the good-dad skipper: sometimes you just have to lose your shit, if only to show the kids you still care.

Ten days after Boston, an appointment was made to sit and talk with Cashman. Things hadn't improved much since the Fenway slaughter: the Yanks had won some games against low-rent teams, then tripped themselves up in ugly losses. Judge, who thought he'd miss only three weeks, hadn't swung a bat by week four. His prognosis was pushed to mid-September. Sánchez was jogging and taking BP, but he too was out till September. Sabathia's knee landed him on the disabled list, Severino's funk stretched into its sixth week, and no one had a clue what was up with Greg Bird, who continued to mark in absent at the plate.

But Cashman bopped in that day wearing a bronze backpack, looking like he'd come from the Governor's Ball. He joked about all the texts backed up on his queue, laughed about a prank he'd played on one of his coaches, and imitated his late great pal Gene Michael when asked about Judge's status. "As Stick would say, 'He's got no *pop*, Cash! No pop *at all* in the wrist!'" Word had it that Judge was training in the pool, swinging underwater without a bat. Cashman said he hoped Judge would be right by Labor Day, but allowed he might not heal up till March. "He told us he'd play with pain, but even a checked swing . . . You never know with these things." He had no news on Sabathia or Clint Frazier, the sweet-hitting kid who'd missed two months with slow-to-heal concussions: "It wasn't supposed to be a long-term issue, but I guess it took a turn for the worse."

The medical updates done, it was time to press Cashman: What had *happened* to his Yanks these last six weeks? (Since June 24, they'd gone 22-21. The Red Sox were 34-9.) He conceded that the team had scuffled a while, but said, "We haven't had our big guns in the lineup," and, "A couple of the good young guys" had hit a wall. "Gleyber's in a rough patch, but he *is* an All-Star and was leading for Rookie of the Year." Same deal for Sevy: "It might be a function of youth. You forget he's twenty-four 'cause he's been here a while, but there's always some regression that pops up. The first half, he was lights out every time, and we know that his velo's still there." Cashman swiveled in his seat, checking Severino's numbers on Statcast. "Yup: average fastball's 97 this year. Last year, 96.8." He entertained the notion that Sevy was tipping pitches, but said that that was "true of a lot of guys — and if you have elite stuff, they still can't hit you." Finally, on Bird, he admitted to being baffled. "He's far enough past surgery [on his right ankle] that you wonder what's going on. He says he's pain-free, so is it a matter of not having the strength back? Frankly, we don't know — but he's our first baseman."

Cashman was prodded on what *else* he thought was missing. Were his hitters squeezing the bats too tight with runners in scoring position? Were they too reliant on three-run homers and crooked-number rallies? How about those losses to the O's and Rays — was a lack of focus the issue? Cashman, to his credit, answered each question, but often not the one that was actually posed. At fifty-one, he's much more a boxer than an ex-player; his rope-a-dope skills are spot-on. Every time you think you've got him pinned in a corner, he snaps your head with a counter shot and brings the fight to you. The thrust of his answers was that we had it all wrong: The week-to-week drama didn't matter. What *really* mattered was where the Yanks went from here, not where they stood today.

"Take a step back and forget what Boston's doing — it's a pretty special group we've got," Cashman said. "We believe we're heavyweights, but we took a shot in Boston and have a little jelly-leg now. Still, take a look at our projected record and where we are with the wild card. If you'd told me before the season that I'm guaranteed the playoffs, I'd have said, '*Fuck yeah*, man.'"

"Really? Folks were projecting you in the World Series. Don't you *have* to go deep in October?"

Scoffing: "Nope. Don't care what folks project."

"So you could lose the wild-card game and still feel you're moving in the right direction?"

He gave that bullfighter stare of his, as in, *Really? You gonna go there with me?*

"Do I think our roster's improved this year? Yes, I do. Do I think our operations are better? Yes. Does that guarantee anything in October? No. Last year we took out the Cleveland Indians, a team that was rated better than us. Then we took Houston to seven games in a series they were heavily favored. Doesn't matter if you're the first or second wild-card team: you have a chance to be the last team standing."

At that point, he jumped rhetorical horses, likening a baseball season to racing's Triple Crown. "You got the Preakness, the Derby, and the Belmont. The last one's a marathon, the other two are sprints. That's why it's so hard to win 'em all: it takes a horse with a lot of different skills. What *I* care about now is the second and third season" — meaning the divisional and championship round, then the World Series. Bos-

ton was "on fire," he said, and "all respects are due there," but "hopefully
they peak" before October. And anyway, "the *seventh* month is a different deal": a short track with strong clubs bunched together. "At the end
of the day, the team that wins *that* one is the group that gets healthy and
hot."

Next on the list of questions was Boone. How was Cashman feeling
now about his hire in light of these last few weeks and, well, Boston?

"*Very* thankful," he said flatly. "Today, August 16, I feel as good as
I did when the interviews finished" (the previous fall). "He's already
a good manager, and he's going to be really good. I hope he's here ten
years. Or more."

"Right. But in situations where the team is struggling, is it necessary
that he find another voice? Maybe call a meeting, show a different side?"

"Different *how*?"

"Well, not to knock the food cart over, but —"

"You're asking would I want him to turn over the *spread*? Yeah, if
it's part of his personality. But I don't know if that's in there and I don't
care. There's strength in *not* doing something fake because you're getting pressure from the press. His players count on him having a steady
hand, and that's the trust factor there."

For three months, he said, Boone's team took the field feeling like it
couldn't lose. Then "the perfect storm blew through his office": Sánchez,
Judge, Tanaka, and Torres all missed lengthy stretches, and a slew of lingering hurts (Frazier, pitcher Tommy Kahnle, Sabathia, et al.) robbed
him of roster depth. Currently, Stanton was nursing a hamstring, so
Neil Walker and Shane Robinson were forced to play right. Doctors
had just sidelined Ellsbury for the year, so *he* couldn't spell Hicks or
Gardner. Consequently, Boone had to walk the line between "competing and protecting his guys" — giving Gardner a night off in game 4
against Boston, or sitting Walker a day just as he caught fire. "People
don't know what goes on behind the scenes with players. The trainer

might be telling us, 'Back off or we'll have a problem.' Sometimes you lose the battle to win a war."

Which segued, sort of, to his deadline moves. Cashman was saluted for his pickups of J. A. Happ and Lance Lynn, starters who could carry him into October—or through it, if luck allowed. Happ had been a godsend in his first four starts, winning all four with a two ERA and giving Boone length each time. But Lynn had been the bigger surprise: a last-second grab in the checkout lane, he'd made three starts, all quality wins. In exchange for the two starters, Cashman had cleaned out his closet. He sent the ill-starred Brandon Drury and Quadruple-A type Billy McKinney to Toronto in the deal for Happ; traded old friend Tyler Austin, who needed a change of scenery, and Luis Rijo, a Development League reliever, to the Twins for Lynn; and made three other moves to declutter. Off went end-of-the-pen types Adam Warren to Seattle, Chasen Shreve and Giovanny Gallegos to St. Louis, and Caleb Frare, a Double-A reliever, joined the White Sox. In return, Cashman freed up multiple roster spots—and reaped a fortune in international slot money.

In baseball, as in most sports, good teams go through cycles. If they're lucky, they get a five-year window to win a couple of pennants (and maybe a Series). Then their premier vets get old, their homegrown stars hit the free-agent market, and salary constraints dictate who they sign and who they don't. Nor can they reload through a channel of cheap talent. The annual amateur draft is weighted progressively: the bad and middling teams get to pick before the good teams and grab the best high school and college kids. That leaves the strong clubs one viable option: the international amateur market. But there too, hard limits apply.

In its quest for "comparative parity," MLB imposes stringent caps on what teams can pay teens from Cuba (and Venezuela, the Dominican Republic, and the other Latin countries). Thanks to the recent collective bargaining agreement (CBA)—the worst deal in decades for the players — clubs are allowed to spend $4 million to $6 million *total* in a calendar year. That's a far piece from the days of José Abreu ($68 million from the White Sox in 2013), Yasiel Puig ($42 million, Dodgers, in '15), and Yoán Moncada ($31 million, Red Sox, '15). To be fair, if you're twenty-five or older and have played in a recognized professional league for six or more years, you can still get an Abreu/Puig–type deal. But why the union didn't advocate for younger prospects is hard to comprehend — and beyond the scope of this book.

Of course, *all* CBAs offer loopholes to the rich, and no one works those seams smarter than Cashman. The rules allow him — for the moment at least — to acquire *other people's money* in trades. In 2018, he netted the maximum, $3.75 million, in those deadline dumps of spare relievers. That brought his total budget to almost $9 million, of which he'd already spent $5 million. He wasted not a second in spending the rest. On July 29, he signed Osiel Rodriguez, a sixteen-year-old Cuban who stands six-three and throws 97 from various arm slots. (Think El Duque Hernández, but half his age and bearing a legitimate birth certificate.) Three days later, he bagged Alexander Vargas, also sixteen, a Cuban shortstop with limitless range who runs a 6.5 sixty. Between them, he paid out $3.3 million — and restocked his talent pond.

"In *this* world order, with the rules that hinder you, the only way to improve is to max out," said Cashman. "We're projected to win a hundred games [in 2018], so we're not picking high in the draft. And if we stay healthy the next few years, we're not picking high then either. Now, did I help Seattle with Adam Warren? Maybe. He could come back to haunt us. But my only thought is, *How can I help* us, *and meanwhile take care of the future?*"

The conversation wrapped with the biggest deal he made — and a still bigger deal that went poof. Zach Britton, the closer who once saved sixty straight but who'd missed half of 2018 rehabbing his Achilles tendon, came over from the Orioles, at a price. Cashman paid with kids he had real plans for — Dillon Tate, the whippet lefty from the Carlos Beltrán deal, and Cody Carroll, a find in the 2015 draft who'd become a lights-out short man stashed in Scranton. (Josh Rogers, the third piece, was a fifth or sixth starter likely ticketed for the Rule 5 draft.) Britton had been mostly lousy since the deal — bouncing his bowling-ball sinker in the dirt and walking the eighth and ninth hitters — but would probably get his act together by September and be another nuclear warhead in late innings.

"We evaluated the market as being weak in starters, which made us dream, 'Let's reinforce our pen,'" said Cashman. "Again, it's all about run prevention," be it early or late in games. Unable to shake loose a playoff ace, he'd chosen to "close the gap" at the other end. On the subject of aces, it was learned from a source that he'd checked in on Madison Bumgarner. The answer coming back: not available. "They *can't* move him," says our source at the Giants. "He's their Derek Jeter, in so many words." When Bumgarner hits the free-agent market, the Giants "think they can re-sign him." And with Jacob deGrom, the Yankees never got to first. The Mets wouldn't even discuss him.

"Insane," says an inside source. The Mets had "the best trade currency on the market," "a broken-down farm system" that they *had* to fix, and no money to spend on Bryce Harper or Manny Machado over the coming winter. But "instead of creating magic" with deGrom and Syndergaard, "they pulled a Donald Trump and tripled down on what failed the last two years." Upshot: they'd field the "same team next year. Teams came away scratching their heads."

Finally, on the trade that never was: "What about Machado? Were you in?"

Cashman, sighing: "Yeah, we tried."

"Were you close?"

"I thought we were going to wind up with him. But . . ."

He'd reached out to the Orioles and been told by their reps that they wanted "a ton of pitching" back. *Fine,* thought Cashman: he offered them a fair package that included the kids he'd send for Britton. Then, "at the last second, the Orioles pivoted and decided they wanted a position player as the primary." Same old Orioles, in other words: chaos and incompetence in a rich Béarnaise. Meanwhile, they screwed a pair of partners at the trading deadline. When the Dodgers swooped in with a deal the O's preferred, Baltimore never informed the Phils or Brewers. Cashman noted: "I remember talking to the Phillies, like, 'Dude, he's a *Dodger.* They told me two days ago.' But the Philly guy's like, 'What! No way! I'm still talking to them.'"

It was time to wrap up. The Rays were in for a day game, and Cashman wanted to watch first pitch. Tentative plans were made to meet in late October and debrief him about the season.

"Thanks," he said. "But just remember what I told you: that *seventh* month's a very different deal."

7

NIGHT SCHOOL

Nobody wants to cover baseball in August: it's the school-detention month of the regular season. Your friends are at the Cape with their restive kids, or they've stashed them at camp to go hike the Adirondacks and wash down pan-fried trout with a tart rosé. You, on the other hand, are brined in your own juice as you stand there, sweat-soaked, watching BP. The field is a furnace, it's three hours till game time, and the players you need to talk to are sick of your face, having answered the same questions for five months. You know they have nothing to say, and they know you know it. But the game is on the schedule, and so you hover. *Damply.*

Beyond the heat and tedium, the hitters are exhausted. Imagine wielding a sledgehammer for five straight months, with no weekends off or personal days. The act of swinging a bat many, many dozens of times a day is hell on your ligaments and spine alignment. Everything hurts on these guys, especially hips and wrists. There used to be a cure for that — first, greenies and steroids, then Adderall and HGH. Now there's only Red Bull and Tylenol. Neither of those boost one's mood around writers.

The Yankees, more than most, had cause for the August blues: their players kept dropping like flies. While they treaded water till Judge and Sánchez returned, down went Sabathia with a flare-up of arthritis. A week later, it was Didi, upended on the base paths and sidelined with a badly bruised heel. The day after Didi, Aroldis Chapman motioned that he had to come out of a game. All year long, he'd battled inflammation in his left, or push-off, knee. "Previously, I've been able to manage it," he said, "but the pain was more than usual." The Yanks placed him on the ten-day disabled list. They weren't optimistic that he'd be back that soon.

In total, seventeen Yankees had hit the DL since the team broke camp in March. Eight were on the current list, including three who were done for the year (Ellsbury, Montgomery, and Heller). Clint Frazier, who was still in concussion protocol, hadn't even resumed "baseball activities." Judge's wrist was worse than the Yanks were letting on, and Stanton (hamstring) was a bad step away from being lost for a month. The deepest lineup in baseball now had the density of a Pringle: essentially, it was Andújar, Stanton, and . . . stand by.

In addition, Gardner hadn't hit a lick since May. At thirty-five, he looked, frankly, finished. Bird was a basket case, taking strikes down the middle and chasing balls a foot off the plate. Torres was healthy, but his batting average wasn't. For most of the summer, the Magic Rookie had ridden the interstate, hitting .145 and rolling over sliders instead of slapping them to right for hits. Aaron Hicks, their sixth hitter, had been bumped up to third and in this, his *best* year, was struggling to hit .250, despite his .366 on-base percentage.

One night David Cone was remarking about the run of injuries the Yankees had suffered since June. Cone, who's fifty-five but looks like he could still go an inning if the Yankees made a call to the TV booth, is the best and brightest of the five-too-many analysts who work the team's broadcasts on YES. (Why do the Yanks employ *seven* color men? Because they can, of course.) Cone was asked if he could think of a club as good as this one that had been so undone by bad luck. "Well, yeah, one," he said. "My '87 Mets. Our *whole rotation* was DL'ed that year — including [Rick] Aguilera, the sixth starter." That Mets group aside, though, he couldn't recall the likes of this, particularly in a team so young. "I mean, Judge, Sánchez, Didi, Frazier — they're all just kids, more or less."

But still, God help them, the Yanks were hanging around, pasting together wins with spit and gristle. They'd gone 15-5 since the catastrophe in Fenway, beating crappy teams and chipping games off the schedule till they — presumably — got whole in September. It's easy to forget how fortune-dependent a sporting season is. You can assemble the best team in the game in December, then watch it turn to ashes in August. Cashman, to his credit, had constructed a roster that took gut-shot after gut-shot and kept coming. These Yankees were a proof-point of his working theorem: *redundancy + talent = playoffs*. No, they weren't fun now, not by anyone's standards. Even the players seemed restless for better days. But you couldn't watch this club put one foot in front of the other and not marvel at its fuck-you toughness. They'd been built to be Mike Tyson, but Mike Tyson had no chin and stayed down when he got clocked. These Yankees got up, and every time they did so, they made you think of Vinny Pazienza. Vinny Paz, the Italian hardhead from the slums of Rhode Island, badly broke his neck in a car crash in '91. Against medical orders — and the pleas of sweet reason — Paz was up and sparring after doctors removed the halo they'd bolted onto his skull in lieu of surgery. He won his first bout back the following year, then beat Roberto Durán, twice, for a super middleweight belt. Now, *that* guy was fun to watch.

Back in the days before the Yankees played on YES and split $600 million a year with their partner, FOX — to be clear, that's the cash flow from just their local TV deal, as distinct from what they earn on broadcasts (much more on this subject in the next chapter) — the team used to air about a hundred games a year on WPIX. A sweet, sleepy station in the New York City market, PIX built its listings around *Gilligan's Island* reruns and the six glorious seasons of *Superman*. On days when the Yankees were sidelined by weather, PIX would run something called *Rainout Theater,* screening gumshoe noir from the forties and fifties or, if they were really feeling charitable, a Marx Brothers flick. Whatever they showed, it was often better than the games, because the Yankees of that era (circa 1965–1975) were mostly awful.

So, rather than recap their August games against the dregs of MLB (after Boston, the Yankees played twenty-seven straight games versus teams with no playoff hopes), we offer our version of *Rainout Theater:* a spirited newsreel, RKO-style, of their rookies in the Gulf Coast League. This selection, however random-seeming, is the furthest thing from it. Those four teams in Tampa are the fruit of Cashman's relaunch — and served as the tide pool for his 2018 Yanks. Sánchez, Severino, Andújar, Torreyes, Jonathan Loaisiga, Luis Cessa, and on and on: all of them came through the finishing school that is the Tampa baseball complex.

Back in 2014, when he hit the reset button, Cashman tasked Gary Denbo, then his director of player development, to radically overhaul the Yankees' minor league program. Between their Gulf Coast rookie teams in Tampa and their two out-of-state, low-A teams, the Yankees have 170 kids in the lower minors, the most of any franchise in the sport. Almost half those kids are graduates of the Yankees' academy in Boca Chica, their hatchery in the Dominican Republic, which was built in 2005. Some were discovered on city sandlots, others in backwoods hamlets that don't appear on any map. Virtually all of them were poor, and quite a number couldn't read. Their instructors at the academy had to teach them grade-school *Spanish* as well as their first phrases in English. The goal, beyond honing their baseball skills and filling out their frames with robust meals, was to raise their functioning to at least a sixth-grade level before they left the island for America.

Between 2005 and 2014, those kids from the DR got to Tampa and were essentially cut adrift. They had to learn, on their own, how to order a meal at Denny's, figure out the exchange rate when they sent their *centavos* home, and try to apply for a Social Security number. It didn't help that some of their teammates came from places poorer than theirs. "I've had kids come through from [rural] Venezuela who hadn't even seen *electricity,*" says Melissa Hernandez. Hernandez, a Dominican native the Yanks recruited in 2014, is their head instructor in Tampa. She's one of twenty-five full- and part-time teachers hired by the team in the last four years. "When they get here, they're lost," she says. "They've never used a computer or gotten cash [from an ATM]." *Those* things are in her curriculum too. She's as much the players' den mom as their mentor.

Not all of the 170 kids in Low-A ball need this sort of reboot. Roughly a quarter of that group are US prospects chosen in the amateur draft. Those kids arrive here in June, get fitted and kitted by the equipment squad, then ship out to short-season ball. The ones who stay in Tampa are the international signings, many of whom hail from countries or territories without academies (including Venezuela, Colombia, and Puerto Rico, among others). From April 23 to August 6, the Yanks hold intense remedial classes at their sprawling baseball campus in Tampa. Called the Himes Complex, it's a half-mile down the road from George M. Steinbrenner Stadium. There are five adjoining diamonds for intrasquad games; a two-story watchtower from which Kevin Reese, the current director of player development, Eric Schmitt, his assistant director of development, and various scouts, trainers, coaches, and coordinators can track the players on all diamonds; and a newish field house that's the rocket factory for assembling next-gen Yankees.

On the first floor of the field house, which was refurbished two years ago, there's a hangar-sized space that's both a fitness center and a sports-performance clinic. One end of it looks like a flagship Gold's:

aisle after aisle of free weights, Smith machines, ellipticals, and climbers, plus devices whose functions no layman could fathom. At the other end is the science lab: indoor mounds and cages where a prospect's every movement — his swing path, his windup, his first step out of the batter's box — is taped and digitized and assessed in real time by analysts sitting at desktops. The Yankees weren't the first club to spend many millions of dollars on biometric equipment and technicians; the Cubs, Dodgers, and Astros beat them to it. But no one has a setup as expansive as this one — or satellite installations at every farm club. That's where Reese and Schmitt come in: from their offices upstairs, they and their six stat techs amass, crunch, and cross-check data from all nine teams in the Yankees' minor league chain. Then Reese sends the data points up to Cashman. The two men talk or text almost every day.

Interviews with Reese and Schmitt were set up separately as the Tampa season wound down. Reese, an ex-outfielder and Yankee product who played till '07 in their organization, presents as a general-manager-in-waiting: polished, muscular, adroit in all departments. Schmitt, a taller man, has the build of a former pitcher; he and Reese were roommates in the minors. In their respective offices, which look exactly alike — all Yanks execs have Cashman's battleship desk — they talked about the massive ramp-up in Tampa since the relaunch of 2014.

"When I started here, I *thought* we had a big department — it was eighteen staffers," said Reese, who coordinates everything from the mental-conditioning program to the hiring and firing of coaches. "Now it's in the hundreds, and all the stuff you're seeing is either new or from the last three years." Like every young capo under Cashman, Reese, who's forty, practically race-walked through the Yankees' system. He started as a pro scout in 2008, quickly jumped to regional chief, then served as Denbo's assistant of player development. That upward mobility is one of the charms of these new-age Yankees: if you're good, there's a fast lane to the top.

"When I was a player, I'd look up north and see we'd traded for Gary Sheffield or signed Hideki Matsui, and here I am, a center fielder in Triple-A thinking, *When am I gonna get* my *shot?*" Now, says Reese, when he talks to the players down here, he tells them their opportunity is bright. "Just look at our parent club: all those good kids have broken through." Even someone like Carlos Mendoza, who'd started as a coach with the Staten Island Yankees and managed the Gulf Coast affiliate, is now the Yankees' infield coach.

Each year Cashman sends a clear directive south: "We need to be better in every aspect." Whatever Reese and Schmitt ask for — more scouts, more equipment, a quant embedded with each team — Cashman goes to Hal and gets the funding. Schmitt demurred when asked how much Hal had spent here, but offered that he'd "been over quite a bit." Yes, the Invisible Owner — Hal Steinbrenner — visited the complex often to "watch games, ask about prospects, and about anything else we might need," said Schmitt. Hal had bought hotels for two of the Low-A teams to live in during the season; paid for suites in the hotels he didn't own so kids could cook meals, not eat fast food; hired nutritionists to personalize each player's intake; and put out spa-style spreads three times a day. "I played with guys that the only thing they could do in English was order McDonald's," says Reese. As they climbed the system, "they continued to make questionable food choices because that's what they knew how to do."

But with all their new hardware and content upgrades, the one thing Reese and Schmitt seemed proudest of was the work being done in the Yankee classrooms. There, on the first and second floors of the field house, is where the reformation happens: the morphing of unschooled, ballplaying teens into textbook Yankees. "It's our focus and our goal, for the players who go north to be able to do their interviews in English," says Reese.

It begins where you least expect it to: with viewings of the old sitcom

Friends. Watching on a projection screen at the front of the room, a dozen or so men with a fledgling grasp of English try to find the levity in six neurotic New Yorkers seeking romance without commitments (or STDs). Though it surely wasn't intended to, the series could have been scripted for the purpose of teaching young players civics. The actors talk slowly, enunciate clearly, and speak the sort of flat-earth English you're never going to hear in the Bronx. For the players' benefit, the show is subtitled — in *English*. That way, they learn to read what they're hearing, and to think in cadenced phrases. Most importantly, the show transmits the values these new-age Yanks espouse: friendship, teamwork, and living in peace with buddies who badly out-earn you.

That, at least, was the theme of the episode being shown to them that day. Three of the friends had money and three didn't; tensions, if not hilarity, ensued. When it ended, Melissa Hernandez clicked on the lights and asked, "How much did you guys understand?"

Several of the players rubbed their eyes; it was the end of another long workday. They'd been playing or training since 8:00 a.m., and here it was going on dusk. They responded to her questions in fractured English, then filled in two-page quizzes on what they'd watched. The general tenor of the quiz guided their answers: *When you're broke, be honest. Tell your friends you can't go party. Don't lie and spend money you don't have.* Afterwards, they trooped to the culinary classroom to watch a staff chef prepare linguine. The roasted chicken and sautéed veggies over the pasta was dull but healthy fare. They jotted down instructions, sampled the finished dish, then grabbed prepacked dinners and bottled water from a giant fridge.

As they waited for the shuttles to their nearby hotels, Klapisch stopped Argelis Herrera, a six-foot-six Dominican from a flyspeck town called Tenares. Or at least that's what he tells foreigners. Tenares is the only town near him in the DR that's searchable on Google Earth. He actually lives in Arriba, a dirt-floor village where GPS is useless. Nor will you find it by driving around the outskirts. There *are* no roads in those hills. "It's a humble place," he says in Spanish. "You have to walk the last two miles to my house."

Herrera is nineteen, humps it up there at 94, and is working on a slider and change. But he's in his first year at Tampa, and with only a first-grade education when the Yankees signed him, he's far behind his teammates. His father grows fruit to sell at a stall, and if it weren't for baseball, Argelis would be slaving alongside him. He spent his two years at the Yanks' academy in Boca Chica just learning proper Spanish; this is his first real dalliance with English. The good news is that he'll have an honest chance here to refine both his syntax and his slider: the Yankees are extra-patient with these kids. They pay them standard wages for low-A players — about $1,200 a month, in addition to whatever bonus they earned at signing. But the Herreras are given several years to leap to the next level — the Yanks' full-season A-ball team in Charleston, South Carolina.

The numbers, in full candor, are stacked against them. Of the 170 prospects playing Rookie ball, only a quarter or so will make the jump to the middle rungs of A-ball. And in private conversations, a Yankees official admitted that most of these imports are fodder. "We sign five or ten kids who are stars in their country, and forty or fifty others so they'll have someone to play against once they get here," he says.

The odds of those "other" players having a future in baseball are somewhere between slim and adios. Of the almost three hundred prospects in the Yankees system, maybe 10 percent will reach the majors, and only a fraction of those will stick around long enough to get vested in its pension plan. But for as long as they're in the Yankees' chain, these kids are well served for their time. The Tampa life skills classes are repeated at every level of the minors, prepping players for baseball and beyond. And for all the kids who *don't* make the bigs, the Yankees have a bonus clause: they offer a college scholarship to every prospect who washes out of their system. No matter where they're from or where they pursue a future, the Yankees will pick up the tab for their college degree.

"I'm in touch with thirty or forty guys who went home, and most of them do go on to college," says Hernandez. From there they open their own businesses or go into teaching or other middle-class professions. What they *don't* do is go back to their fathers' farms.

"When I came here, I didn't speak *any* English — none of us did," says Miggy Andújar, the sensational rookie who carried the Yanks through their doldrums for much of August. Signed at sixteen from one of the DR's larger cities, Andújar spent a couple of summers in Tampa before making the jump to Charleston. "But the classes helped me learn, little by little, and I kept learning as I moved up the system. I wouldn't be speaking English today if it weren't for the Yankees." Asked to rate his fluency now, he laughs and says, "So-so." But he insists on speaking English, as does Severino, whose command of the language is superb. "It was hard," says Severino, recounting his time in Tampa. "You're hot, you're tired, you just want something to eat. But the program gets you started so you can have a conversation with your American teammates. That's *really* where you learn English: in the clubhouse. You take what you learn in class and you speak to the American kids. And you don't have to feel embarrassed about making a mistake because no one judges you here."

Typically, class time is two hours long and consists of two subjects a day. Banking and personal finance is taught in a room down the hall, with laptops at every station. There, players learn about budgeting, practice tracking expenses on debit cards, and calculate what they hope to save on their modest incomes. There's a course in nutrition that's reinforced daily by the food choices offered downstairs. Let other clubs serve their kids chicken tenders and whatever's on sale at Sam's Club. The Yankees feed their prospects like Olympic hopefuls. That's part of the retooled culture under Cashman: eating, like fitness, is a year-round sport — so don't even *think* of reporting back here next spring with 20 percent body fat. And then, of course, there are the mock media sessions where the players are grilled under pressure. "We know these guys are gonna have to deal with that, so we put them in situations, see how they handle it, then talk about how they can improve," says Reese.

Finally, there's a class in certain hard-knock facts — but one that isn't taught by team instructors. "We have Tampa police officers come in once a month to tell these guys what they can and cannot do," said Hernandez. "Number one, you *can't* do things on a date here that might happen if you were back home — there's laws against that here." Forcible touching, drunken advances, anything over the line can mean jail time and deportation. Other career-killers: drinking beer on porches, driving while impaired, and throwing punches in bars. "I don't know how it was before I got here," says Hernandez, "but in *my* four years, not one kid's been in trouble. So I guess it's working."

As for Herrera, the six-six righty, he's clearly gotten the message. On the mound, he's as raw as a prospect can be (seventeen walks in seven relief innings pitched), but he's such a physical standout that Reese and Schmitt will give him all the time he needs. He's built like Dellin Betances and, like most big pitchers, will need longer to perfect his mechanics. Where he's making his surest strides is in the classroom: he pays close attention, asks pointed questions, and preps like his future depends on it.

"He has *such* an eagerness to succeed — you just have to teach him how," says Hernandez, who doesn't hide her rooting interest in Herrera. Every day he shows her that "he wants to be someone," and what more can you ask from a kid? He has the body, the arm, and the mindset to win, and the Yankees grade all of those things. There's a reason their phenoms who do make the majors don't flip bats like José Bautista and big-league it around the bases after homers. They're taught at every rung to be dignified adults who happen to wear pinstripes to work.

These Yanks don't flame opponents, don't bring out TMZ, and don't down-talk teammates in the press. The Yankees scout like crazy, sign kids of good character, then give them every chance to become their best selves. And that's how you build a killer franchise these days: you grow it from the subsoil up.

8

NOTHING PERSONAL, IT'S STRICTLY BUSINESS

R andy Levine has a favorite George Steinbrenner story, or at least one that makes him laugh each time he tells it. Understand that Levine still loves the man and misses him every time he comes to mind. But you don't get to where he's gotten in life without doing right by a good yarn. Those stories are Levine's war pay for being president of the New York Yankees, a job that makes him feared and, in some parts, loathed — and utterly indispensable to his team.

However you feel about him — and your view of Levine will vary, depending on whether he's crushed you in a deal — there's no half-stepping his achievements. He is the Zelig of baseball's power elite, a man who's been in at the birth of many of its biggest milestones since 1991. He was the chief negotiator for MLB during the strike years of '94–'95, when he brokered the collective bargaining agreement that brought the sport into the twentieth century. He struck the notorious deal with then-commissioner Fay Vincent to let Steinbrenner back into baseball. (Google it — it's well worth your time.) He got the new Stadium built over hellacious resistance; put the YES Network, the first team-owned regional sports net, on the air to earn billions for the Yankees; and cofounded a company called Legends Hospitality to sell food and drink at the ballpark. In its ninth year of business, Legends is now valued at $1 billion and services dozens of stadiums and convention sites. Not a bad obit, haters and all.

But Levine, who's sixty-three, is talking about George — his boss, best buddy, and chief tormentor. "I was the first call he made almost every day, and often the last one too," he says, getting a little tight in the throat. "But there were days when he wouldn't speak to me, or called me everything under the sun: a 'dope,' a 'failure,' *'you're on the bubble, Levine!'* Which was fine, 'cause those weren't one-way conversations. I'd fucking unload on him too."

And so the story begins. "I was in LA on business, 1991, and they didn't have beepers in those days. So I'm at LAX to take the red-eye back, and I hear over the speaker, 'Randy Levine, come to the courtesy phone.' That was George: he could reach out and find you wherever you were in the world. He says, 'Hey, buddy, where are you?' I said, 'Where *am* I? You just called me at LAX!' He says, 'Right, right — hey, look, I gotta see you, what time you landing? Come straight to my hotel, 8:00 a.m.'"

At the time, Levine was a partner at a prestige law firm and had no business ties to the Yanks. But he'd been friends with George since the early '80s, when the two men met in New York's power circles. He showed up at the Regency, where George kept a luxe apartment, to entertain an offer he couldn't refuse. One year prior, George had been suspended from baseball for his payoffs to a sad-sack gambler named Howie Spira. But what George hadn't grasped then was that his expulsion by Vincent was *permanent,* unlike the two-year whack he got in the 1970s for funneling dark money to Richard Nixon. "So George says, 'I made a bad mistake and you gotta help me. I think I got screwed on that deal,'" says Levine.

Levine accepted, but extracted harsh conditions, only one of which is printable here. "I told George, 'If I get you back, I want to be your outside counsel and charge you a *lot* of money.'" George agreed to all terms, and Levine and his law firm partner, Arnie Burns, went to work on Vincent. They filed a motion with MLB's executive council, alleging that Vincent had denied George due process. Then they recruited other team owners who were furious at Vincent for various reasons (among them, Jerry Reinsdorf, White Sox owner, and Bud Selig, Brewers owner). "So anyway, long story short, pressure was building from the other owners, and Vincent was forced to make a deal with us," says Levine.

That, at any rate, is Levine's recollection. Vincent's is somewhat different. "Horseshit," he harrumphs over the phone from Vero Beach, Florida, where he and his wife keep a winter home. "George was dead in the water; he had no legal recourse. But I decided [on further reflection] that the proper punishment was two years."

However that compromise came to pass, Levine was eager to convey it to his client. "By this point, it's July and the [1992] Olympics in Barcelona, and George was there with the USOC," Levine continues.

At the time, Steinbrenner was vice chairman of the US Olympic Committee. "But no one knows where to find him, so I leave a message with the committee to have George call me back. Now, it's 2:00 a.m., and George calls me, *screaming*: 'What the fuck are you chasing me all over Spain for!' I said, 'I got great news. The commissioner is announcing tomorrow that you're gonna be reinstated March 1!' 'March 1!' he says. 'Fuck you, Levine! It shoulda been *January 1!*' and hangs up."

As with a lot of Levine's stories, though, there's a second punch line coming. Unbeknownst to all but his closest friends, Levine is a passionate defender of animals. He has a farm outside the city that is home and haven for three abandoned horses, six rescued dogs, and one truculent mule that he and his wife, Mindy, saved from certain death. At their New York apartment, they live with the six dogs, who *must* be walked by sunup, "or there's gonna be serious issues in my place." Four hours after George slammed the phone down on him, Levine got off the elevator with his dogs . . . and found the lobby of his building carpeted in flowers.

"For you," said the concierge, handing him a card with two first-class plane seats to anywhere in the world. The attached note was addressed to Mindy, saying—more or less—*Thank you for putting up with Randy all these years!* "Classic George," says Levine, misting up again. "A great, wonderful guy, but it was hard for him to say 'thank you.'"

Or, apparently, "sorry."

Thus was Levine inducted into Steinbrenner's sanctum, which, for all practical purposes, meant his family. The Steinbrenners are as close — and close-mouthed — a brood as has ever loved a man of George's bluster. His widow Joan and their four children (Hal, Hank, Jessica, and Jennifer) are almost never glimpsed in public; it took eight months of pushing to get in front of Hal, the silent-movie star of this book. Once Levine was in, though, he was in all the way, and not just as George's consigliere. From 2000 on, when he left his job with the city administration (he was then the deputy mayor for economic development, his third, and last, position under Rudy Giuliani) to become George's adjutant general, he has either spearheaded or consulted on every major decision George or his loved ones have made.

One of his favorite stories — and certainly the most stunning — is set in the years before he joined the Yankees. In 1998, George almost sold the Yankees to Chuck and Jim Dolan, the father-son moguls who owned the New York Knicks and Rangers; the building those teams played in (Madison Square Garden); and, most crucially, the MSG Network. There was a long and amicable history between George and Chuck Dolan, going back to their city of origin, Cleveland. The two men did their first deal in 1979 for the rights to show the Yanks on a cable network called SportsChannel, a subsidiary of Cablevision.

It was the first real money the Yanks made from broadcast rights. In the sixties and early seventies, they actually *paid* to be on the radio, giving WMCA $5,000 per game while earning peanuts off their TV deal with WPIX. George re-upped with Chuck in the early eighties, but wrote an escape hatch for himself into that contract. He reserved the right to exit the deal for one very special reason: to found his own regional sports network. "Since the day I first met him [in the early eighties]," says Levine, "he never stopped talking about it. He just *knew* that's where the real money was, and that it would get bigger over the years."

Chuck Dolan, who's ninety-one now but still a media baron (his portfolio includes MSG, AMC, and a brace of other channels), was a mentor and role model for George. In the sixties, Dolan founded Sterling Manhattan, the first cable channel in the world. Several years later, he created HBO, the first premium channel in the world. He eventually spun those off to Time Life, Inc., and used the money to launch Cablevision on Long Island. In 1989, Bob Gutkowski, president of the MSG Network, struck a landmark $486 million deal with George for the exclusive Yankees local television rights until 2000. This unprecedented contract moved baseball away from the pay cable model to basic cable for the first time in major league baseball history.

Then, through a slurry of mergers and acquisitions in the early 1990s, Dolan and one of his sons, Jim, took over MSG in 1995. But the cable deal with the Yankees was still in effect through 2000. In sum, MSG was still paying $50 million annually to televise Yankees games. Meanwhile, George and Chuck continued to try and hash out an eventual sale of the Yankees to the Dolans in 1998.

That $50 million annuity essentially rescued the Yankees, says a senior team official. The Yanks were a bad team then and getting worse by the minute as they entered a period unfairly known as the Stump Merrill era. (Alas, poor Stump: he managed for only a year and a half, but the stink of those seasons endures.) George had been banned from baseball, Andy Hawkins threw a no-hitter in Chicago and *lost,* and only seagulls showed up to watch the action, slugging it out with rodents for hot-dog buns. But that twelve-year deal with Dolan soft-scrubbed their losses and gave George, once reinstated, the needed cash to go out and chase free agents (Jimmy Key, Wade Boggs, and Danny Tartabull, to start the party). For George, it was found money that no one else had and that no team in the National League could even get a percentage of till the landmark labor agreement of '95, when, for the first time, rich clubs were forced to share revenue with small-market clubs.

But back to the pending sale of the Yankees to Chuck Dolan in '98. Besotted with Dolan's brilliance, George wanted to sell him 80 percent of the team for the price of $800 million. For his part, he'd keep 20 percent of the Yanks and gain two more clubs in the bargain: Chuck would name George the operating partner of . . . *the Yankees, the Knicks, and the Rangers.* (Several executives who were party to those talks have confirmed — on tape, if not on the record — that those were the terms of sale.) Oh, how the gag lines write themselves when you imagine George telling the then-Knicks coach, Jeff Van Gundy, *You're on the bubble, Van Gundy!* or berating Neil Smith, the builder of a Rangers roster that won its first Cup in fifty-four years, *What the hell have you won for me lately?*

Chuck Dolan prized the Yankees, but wanted something else besides: to air their games for nothing on MSG. This was smack in the middle of the Core Four's run — two trophies won, two more to follow shortly — and their ratings on MSG were breaking records. Dolan's buyout of George and his minority partners wouldn't come cheap in '90s dollars: that $800 million more than doubled the highest price paid for any team in baseball history. (The record to that point was held by the Dodgers, bought by Rupert Murdoch for $311 million.)

But Chuck Dolan's genius was for seeing the future, and the future was cable carriage fees. "He owned the cable rights to all seven teams [in the New York area] and knew the fans would pay a premium to watch at home," says Levine. A premium, for those fans *still* watching at home, means ever-increasing monthlies — till infinity. The $50 million a year Dolan was paying the Yankees would double in just the next four years. So too the value of the Yanks themselves. Worth $800 million then, they're priced at $4 billion now. Except that Dolan — *Jim* Dolan — killed the deal, say Yankee sources.

"Jimmy wanted to run everything, including the Yanks, and he wasn't gonna answer to George," says a lawyer close to the talks whom we can't name. (Jim Dolan's response — in total — to these assertions: "We have different recollections of what happened.") For months on end, there were meetings between the parties, "Jimmy and Hal [Steinbrenner], Jimmy and Steve Swindal [George's then-son-in-law], but it blew hot and cold," says a source. In the end, "Chuck chose to back out of the deal, because he always deferred to Jimmy for some strange reason."

But the Dolans weren't done looking gift horses in the mouth. Two years later, Levine was named the Yanks' president and given a punch list by George: "I had to build him a Stadium, get a network up and going, and bring in new streams of revenue — yeah, *that's* all," says Levine, who laughs loudly and often once he's on a roll.

So out he went to meet George's new best friends: the guys who'd just bought the New Jersey Nets. Lew Katz and Ray Chambers, local industrialists who'd also bought the New Jersey Devils, had joined with George to form YankeeNets for the purpose of getting a network on-air. Their first idea was to partner with MGM on a station called the Americana Network. Its proposed lineup: Yankees and Nets games with — *wait for it* — musicals from the 1940s. Or, as it might have become known to certain middle-aged men, "Rainout Theater" every day!

Alas, George's relationship with Katz and Chambers "went sour pretty quick," says Levine. "George tells me, 'Go get someone else to build the network.'" Combing his Rolodex, Levine called up Joe Ravitch and Gerry Cardinale, who were bankers at Goldman Sachs. Over drinks at the Four Seasons, the three men hatched a plan, sketching it on a cocktail napkin. Goldman Sachs would front the cash to pay George $90 million a year while the network got on the air in the tri-state market. In exchange, the investment bank would own roughly a one-third stake in YES, as the channel would be known going forward.

But before they could launch the station, they had to break with the

Dolans, who controlled the team's rights for two more years. "So we go to Chuck and Jimmy and say the following: 'You guys have a network, we don't know how to do anything, so we'll sell you 50 percent of [what would become YES],'" says our source. But Jimmy "didn't want to let us out of our rights," and both sides wound up suing each other. Eliot Spitzer, the attorney general, got involved, says Levine: "He banged heads and threatened an antitrust suit if the Dolans didn't settle." Eventually, the parties went to arbitration and "we ended up paying $30 million so Jimmy could build his practice facility in the suburbs," says Levine.

Leaving the room, George and Chuck exchanged handshakes and snippets of chummy trash talk. As they parted ways, though, Chuck looked at George and said, "Congrats on your deal, but you'll never get carried [on-air]."

George, per our sources, glared back at him and said, "We'll see about that, Chuck. We'll see."

So George had his freedom to cut deals with other carriers—but no real content to put on-air. In the summer of 2001, the YES Network existed only as a line item in courthouse papers. George told Levine to hire a program executive who could quickly build or rent large production quarters, hire several dozen veteran TV staffers, and fill a 24-hour day with original product 365 days a year. Oh, and one more thing: that person, whoever it was, had exactly five months before going live.

Levine's first phone call was to John J. Filippelli, a New York sports-programming legend. Brooklyn-born and -raised—his first job as a kid was selling franks and Cokes at Yankee Stadium—Filippelli had a quarter-century of experience producing the *Game of the Week* for NBC. (He also produced the World Series for several networks, as well as Super Bowls, Olympics, and Wimbledons.) "Flip," as he's known by practically everyone in the business, had been friends with

Steinbrenner since the early '80s and was up for the challenge Levine brought him. It was, he says, "a chance to change the landscape of sports TV": build an entire platform around a baseball team and film each of its games with playoff-sized crews, putting ten cameras around the field. (The norm for the regular season then was four.) George gave Flip everything he needed to do that — except, of course, the time to do it sanely.

"Looking back now, my advice is: if living a long life is important to you, don't ever try to put a network together in five months," says Filippelli. "I had no infrastructure, no producers, no mobile units, no nothing. Just a yellow pad, a pen, and my imagination." He signed his YES contract on September 10, 2001. The horrors of the following morning stopped him cold. "No one in New York City wanted to come to work; they were in shock, they were grieving. By Christmas, I was asking myself if we were going to make it." Compounding the problem was his own inexperience: he'd never created content before. "I mean, what did I know about that stuff — I couldn't even program my VCR. But Levine said, 'Don't worry. You'll figure it out.'"

So Filippelli consulted his past. He'd liked *Biography* as a kid, and also the sudsy program *This Is Your Life*. Presto change-o: *Yankeeography* and *Center Stage* were created. He called his friends at MLB and asked them to case their vault for tapes of old Yankee games. Forthwith, *Yankee Classics*. Then he sat with George and presented his list on a slip of paper. George looked at the sheet and said, "What's 'NE'?" "It means, 'Not Enough,'" said Filippelli. "We need to fill more airtime."

GEORGE: "What about those two guys?"

FLIP: "What two guys?"

GEORGE: "The ones in the afternoon. On the radio."

FLIP: "Who, Mike and the Mad Dog?"

GEORGE: "Yeah, those two. Get 'em."

Filippelli was stunned: simulcasting sports radio shows was still in its infancy. But that radio call-in format had printed money for Don Imus and Howard Stern, so why wouldn't it work for a couple of smart curmudgeons who barked at their callers and at each other? "Just like that, George gave me five and a half hours of content a day — right off the top of his head."

Flip still needed someone to call the Yankee games. Initially he thought he'd be able to poach Bob Costas — till he caught a glimpse of his schedule. "He could only do six games a year, and I needed a workhorse who showed up every day and loved the grind." It struck him that he had a guy by that description at hand: not the mellifluous John Sterling, who did the Yankee radio calls, but his longtime radio partner Michael Kay. Kay, an ex-reporter who looked and sounded like the Bronx, had earned a chance to make the big leap. He'd been pointed in this direction since his Hunts Point boyhood, when, as a teen in the '70s, he walked the twenty blocks to watch the Yanks from general admission. "I'm the kid who sat in the upper deck and rooted for Horace Clarke and Jerry Kenney," he says before going on-air one weekday night. "All I ever wanted was to be the Yanks' announcer, though I sounded like Vinnie Barbarino. I'm a fan who got a chance to be in the booth."

Kay, who's fifty-seven and the married father of two, had been a Yankees beat guy for the *Post* and *News* who wisely cultivated Billy Martin. He broke story after story of Billy's turmoil with George, which was the great, botched romance of New York sports. Kay had an eye for clubhouse intrigue and an ear for what his readers wanted to know. He brought that affinity to the booth with him: a clairaudient sense of what his viewers thought and said, even as they were thinking and saying it. That's how you get to be the TV voice of the New York Yankees: by being the voice of the people who watch them nightly.

Filippelli caught lightning when he took a flyer on Kay, who has become an institution with Yankees fans. He isn't as smooth as Gary Co-

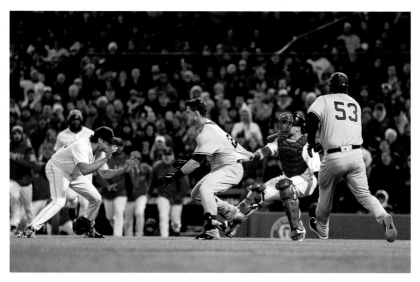

The Red Sox and Yankees were officially at war again in 2018.

Aaron Judge: all smiles and a limitless horizon.

Aaron Boone: the great communicator.

Miguel Andújar: the lineup's secret weapon.

Gleyber Torres goes yard.

Andújar gets his water bucket baptism.

Aaron Judge and Giancarlo Stanton: power times two.

Giancarlo Stanton says hello to the Bronx.

CC Sabathia, clubhouse leader.

Aaron Judge shows off that vertical leap.

Aaron Judge's message to pitchers: don't tread on me.

Aroldis Chapman dials up another high-90s heater.

Masahiro Tanaka, the master of illusion.

Gary Sánchez releases the kraken.

Luis Severino goes primal after another strikeout.

J. A. Happ stays cool under pressure.

Gary Sánchez and Luke Voit prepare for an airborne forearm bash.

Sabathia in trouble against Boston in the Division Series.

Aaron Judge and Brett Gardner grimly watch the season come to an end.

The ultimate wound: the Red Sox celebrate their ALDS conquest at the Stadium.

Yankees president Randy Levine is at the nerve center of the franchise's business operations.

General manager Brian Cashman in a familiar setting, surrounded by the media.

Cashman is now in his twenty-first year running the Yankees' monolith. *Photo by Alex Trautwig / MLB Photos via Getty Images.*

hen, who does the Mets games on cable, or as ingratiating as Joe Buck, who does the playoffs. But he has something distinctly in the New York vein: a lightness of touch about himself. He cares deeply about the game but knows better than to treat it like scripture. He constantly tweaks his partners, Paul O'Neill and David Cone, pitting their pieties against each other just for the hell of it. That's the Bronx in him talking, the ball-busting you do when you sit in row Y with your pals. It makes for good company in a three-hour game against the godawful KC Royals.

It took Levine three years, and biblical labors, to get YES carried in New York. The ordeal, and its legal knife-fights, pales beside the struggle of getting the new Stadium built.

That project took *nine years* and countless screaming matches between Levine and George, Levine and the City Council, Levine and — well, you name it. He negotiated plans with two mayors and two governors — *before* he agreed to stay put in the Bronx. "We'd met with Woody Johnson [the owner of the Jets] to build a stadium for two teams on the West Side Highway," he says. Those talks dragged on forever before they were finally sunk by political opposition and zoning hassles. After five years, Levine had had enough of the Manhattan snake pit and said to George, "We gotta stay in the Bronx."

That was no small ask: George disdained his team's location and thought it irredeemable by any measure. But eventually he was brought around by Levine and other advisers and agreed to seek a deal on River Avenue. Here, then, was the start of a fresh torment: Levine had to navigate waves of community protest *and* get the land for the new ballpark declared condemned. In the end, after battles with the State Assembly and City Council, Levine won approval for not only a new Stadium but also a Metro North station connecting the ballpark to the 'burbs, major improvements to both the adjacent highway and the two subway stations that served the Stadium, and a sprawling green space on the site of the old Stadium. Actually, that turned out to be twin parks side-by-side: the first a series of baseball diamonds and the other a honeycomb of handball courts, basketball courts, and a soccer field. To this day, they're in high-rotation use by kids in the neighborhood.

But Levine's biggest ask was for the $1.4 billion to build this with the *city's* money. There's an IRS law against raising public funds without incurring federal taxes on those loans. To sidestep that annoyance, Levine contrived with Bloomberg's people for the city to be the owner of the new Stadium. This spared the Yankees hundreds of millions in future taxes and also enabled them to borrow at the municipal rate, saving many millions more in accrued interest. The team now pays the note on its forty-year bond — about $75 million a year, in mortgage and interest — but pays the city neither rent nor a cent from what it earns in the Stadium. Furthermore, it deducts that $75 million from its revenue-sharing bill with Major League Baseball. An annoying but useful note: revenue-sharing, or the "competitive-balance tax," is separate and distinct from the luxury tax. The luxury tax, derived from a complex formula, hits chronic overspenders like the Yankees, Dodgers, and Red Sox for every dollar spent over the threshold. By all means, look that formula up, if you're fresh out of chores or need to distract yourself before a root canal.

"In effect, the other teams are paying a third of our note for the new Stadium," says Levine, referencing the amount the Yanks deduct from the income they report to MLB. He also won concessions in the last collective bargaining agreement that chopped the team's payments to MLB by about $40 million a year. "We've paid by far the most money to MLB since 2002 or whenever," he says. "Thanks to the new rules and the stadium deduction, we dropped from number one to number five in revenue-sharing."

And what did New York's taxpayers get for their $1.4 billion, besides the right to go on claiming the Yankees as theirs? Well, in addition to the new parks and the roughly $80 million that the team is donating, over time, to local nonprofits (for recreational programs and health and wellness programs offered by neighborhood schools), Levine granted the city all the monies from Stadium parking — except there *are* no profits from those spots. In fact, they currently lose money hand over fist, in part because the city spent hundreds of millions of dollars to improve mass transit to the park. To be sure, the neighborhood fared nicely in the deal, getting the two parks and hundreds of subsidized apartments built, with a wave of new developments in the wings. Somewhere down the road, the city will cut its losses and sell those parking structures to developers. For the moment, though, it should probably watch its wallet whenever it talks to Levine. The man has a way of getting what he wants, while making everyone else check their back pocket.

Still, you may be asking: Why a chapter on Randy Levine? Because, in every sense that matters, these new-age Yankees are as much his baby as Hal's and Cashman's. There *is* no massive build-out of the team's infrastructure without the cash he brings in each year. Though the Yankees are privately held and don't release public records, *Forbes* magazine put their revenue at $619 million last year, roughly double the league average of $315 million. According to Mike Ozanian, a managing editor at *Forbes* and the cohost of the magazine's *SportsMoney Show* on YES, those figures do not reflect the "upstream earnings" from their ownership stakes in YES, Legends Hospitality, and the New York City Football Club, which they co-own with Manchester City, the English Premier League champions. "Since the Yanks don't report what they make to the press," Ozanian says, "we have to do a *lot* of private-detective work, using many different sources to compile a number."

Ozanian's staff sifts through documents the team files with New York

State's bond authority. "Those tell us what they grossed in Stadium ticket sales, merchandise, and food-and-drink concessions." (Legends Hospitality, their spin-off company, handles the ballpark's catering business and services its sixty-seven luxury suites.) Ozanian also talks to sports lawyers and investment bankers and with MLB itself to get hold of the Yankees' data streams. In conclusion, says Ozanian, who goes to one game a year and sits in the *Forbes* suite at the Stadium, the Yankees "are the most incredibly lucrative property in the history of sports-entertainment content."

He also points out that George fronted an investors' group that bought the team for $8.8 million — and that "CBS sold it to him [in 1973] for less than they'd actually paid." (One Yanks executive, who *never* speaks to the press, showed us the original bill of sale between George and CBS. Sitting in a cabinet in the executive's office, the typed-by-hand contract has yellowed badly and should probably be displayed in a hermetically sealed case in the Yankees Museum down the hall. The best detail — *by far* — in that document is what George actually put down for his stake. It wasn't a million dollars, or even the $800,000 that's been widely bandied about. No, the check he wrote was for *$80,000*. That was somehow enough to buy Steinbrenner 10 percent of the team and to make him its general managing partner.) Says Ozanian, "This is a classic case study of not only understanding your brand but using that brand to buy and enhance new Yankee-related businesses."

By Ozanian's reckoning, there are four social classes in baseball. There are the filthy rich (the Dodgers, Cubs, Giants, and Red Sox); the middling rich (eleven teams, including the Angels, the Astros, and — somehow — the New York Mets); and the merely rich (everyone else in the game). Then there are the New York Yankees in a bracket all their own. They earn 20 percent more than the second-wealthiest team, have a market value nearly three times the average of the other clubs ($4 billion versus $1.6 billion), and have the second-richest TV deal of any team in baseball, earning $125 million a year. (Additionally, they earn about $100 million a year from the game's national TV deals with FOX, ESPN, and TBS.)

Even after the Yankees sold YES to FOX for almost $4 billion in 2014, they held back 20 percent of it for themselves. YES is now valued at $5 billion, so each year their stake in that lucrative network pays them tens of millions of dollars in dividends. And then there's Legends, the hospitality firm that sells concessions and premium goods for dozens of professional and college teams. Like other Yankees properties, Legends has surged and merged. It partnered first with the Dallas Cowboys, then barreled into the business-convention trade by partnering with New Mountain Capital, a private equity firm. Legends posts annual sales in excess of $700 million, brokers personal-seat licenses for NFL teams, and conducts feasibility studies for new arenas, to name just some of its services.

So, to review the punch list George handed Levine when he joined the team as president in 2000. New stadium? *Check.* Ticket revenues have more than doubled in year-over-year comparisons with the old park, which was actually 20 percent larger. New network? *Check.* YES is a cash cow on steroids (like most cows these days, come to think of it). New revenue sources? *Check* and *double-check.* Aaron Judge's jersey is the biggest seller of the last two years, even excluding those bootleg shirts on River Avenue. (Note to consumers: Most of that stuff isn't licensed, so read the label on the garment closely. Then read it again.) But the best part of all the Yankees' off-site income, including the proceeds from Legends, their dividends from YES, and the New York City Football Club, of which the Yanks own 20 percent? Most of that money isn't subject to revenue-sharing, so the team keeps ninety cents of every dollar those streams deliver.

. . .

George Steinbrenner cared only about winning titles and plowed most of his profits back into player contracts. But these aren't his Yankees, and that isn't their only motive. Hal's focus, *besides* winning, is fielding a durable contender that reaches the playoffs every season, growing his gross revenues on and off the field, and paying robust dividends every quarter to his family and minority partners in the team. Cashman's motives closely mirror Hal's. Though he burns to win a title, Cash is patient about the process. "Did I do everything in my power to give this team a chance?" he says. "If so, I have to be able to live with what happens, which, let's face it, is partly about luck. Who's healthy in October? Who gets hot at the right time? All that stuff matters, and I can't control it."

During the second phase of Joe Torre's tenure, 2001–2007, the Yanks won an average of ninety-eight games a year and finished first in their division six of those seven seasons — but made it to the World Series only twice. (They lost both times: in '01 to Arizona on Mo Rivera's blown save in Game 7, and in '03 to the upstart Marlins in Game 6.) Those other five years were a bitches' brew of bad luck (Joba Chamberlain versus midges in Cleveland), bad karma (the loss in the '04 championship series to Boston's lovable "idiots"), and bad timing. (Alex Rodríguez was the league's Most Valuable Player in the '05 and '07 seasons. His combined playoff record those years: .200 batting average, zero home runs, and one solitary run batted in.)

Cashman built teams that should've won more titles during the Core Four's prime. To this day, he is bothered by that fact. In private, he blames neither A-Rod nor Sheffield, who were mostly awful in those playoffs. Nor does he whine about karma or timing or any of the other vagaries of the game. To the extent that he points a finger, it's at Torre himself, whose leadership in those late years seemed to flag. Cashman won't add to the record on that subject, beyond what he said earlier in this book. But the source of his rancor is clear enough: Torre's 2009 memoir, *The Yankee Years*. In the best-selling book, cowritten by Tom

Verducci, Torre called out a number of ex-Yankees, saying, for instance: "The difference between Kevin Brown and David Wells is that both make your life miserable, but David Wells meant to." Of Carl Pavano, a gifted righty who didn't pitch much for the Yanks after they signed him to a four-year deal (he missed half the '06 season complaining of "bruised buttocks" and the other half recouping from broken ribs sustained when he crashed his Porsche into a truck), Torre wrote: "The players all hated him. It was no secret."

Joe saved his strongest medicine, however, for Cashman. In the book, he complained about the "lack of trust" between them, saying that it spiked after Cashman re-upped in '05 and was granted greater latitude by George. Per Torre, Cashman became overreliant on stats, staffed up his own analytics crew, and discounted Torre's take on roster decisions. But it's Torre's final zinger that stung the worst: his claim that Cashman "betrayed" him "on several fronts" during his last contract sit-down with George. He accused Cash of remaining "neutral" during the session, which was attended by a number of top-line executives. When asked, several of those executives gave a very different take on what transpired at that meeting — and in the years before it.

Per Levine, whose account was seconded by others who bore witness: "Cash was *incredibly* loyal to Joe. He stood up for Joe's job at least twice. George wanted to fire Joe in '06 *and* '07, after we lost to the Tigers and Indians [in the ALDS]. But Cash and Steve [Swindal] talked George out of it — and remember, Steve was gonna be George's successor as managing partner of the Yanks." Per another source who was at the meeting in Tampa, "Brian flew down there a day ahead to ask George to give Joe a hearing. Then he took a late flight back to New York, told Joe he'd gotten him the face-to-face with George, and sat next to him on the plane ride down there."

There were conflicting reports about that meeting. The media said that Torre had been asked to take a pay cut. Several people who were there in Tampa and who heard the terms that Torre turned down said otherwise. Truth was, Torre faced a 33 percent reduction in guaranteed pay, to $5 million, but it was attached to an important clause. "Yes, George offered him $5 million, but with easy incentives that could bring it to $8 million and earn him a second-year extension," says one person who was present. (In 2007, Torre made $7.5 million; his closest competitor was Lou Piniella, who earned $3.5 million to run the Cubs.) "George's pitch was, 'We paid you a premium when you won all those titles, but you haven't won a title in seven years. Still, we don't want you to leave, so we're making you a fair offer here.'"

Torre wanted two years with a stipulation that if he got fired during the 2008 season, his 2009 salary would be paid in full. If he was dismissed after 2008, however, he would receive a buyout for '09. The Yankee hierarchy almost immediately declined. Torre left Tampa and signed a deal with the Dodgers for just over *4 million* a year. LA dropped out of the playoffs each of his three seasons, and Torre quit managing in 2010, having finished out his term. One side note worth inserting: Torre managed three teams before the Yanks' job came along. He ran the Mets for five seasons, the Braves for three, and the St. Louis Cardinals for six. In those fourteen seasons, he won zero pennants, finished 107 games below .500, and was fired by all those clubs.

Most managers with losing records don't get a fourth chance, let alone one with the resurgent Yanks. In his twelve years in the Bronx, Torre brought home six pennants and those four World Series in his first five seasons. But it wasn't Torre who drafted and groomed the Core Four or signed their All-Star subalterns. It was a litany of whip-smart people who came before him — Cashman and Brian Sabean and Stick Michael and many others — and it was George (and Levine) who made the money available to bulk up the lineup with "big boppers," as Torre called Sheffield, A-Rod, Giambi, et al. Nevertheless, says Levine, "Torre thought he made George Steinbrenner, when it was George who made Joe Torre."

Levine, who admits to a certain fondness for Torre while conceding that he didn't finish Joe's book ("You know, it just felt like . . . this is Joe, and Joe was always about Joe"), says that George didn't mind the credit Torre claimed for managing those title teams. What George resented was "Joe cutting him *out* of the credit, along with everyone else. George was always a 'we' guy, not a 'me' guy, and Torre thought he'd grown bigger than George."

One last note on the fallout from Torre's book. In January of '09, days before its publication, a bootleg copy was obtained by the *Post,* where it made a very big splash. That was the week of the annual Baseball Writers' Association dinner. Cashman showed up to it and was ambushed by the press about the charges Torre levied in the book. Cashman told reporters that he didn't know anything about a rift and hadn't yet read the book. Then he left the event and rang up Torre, who was vacationing in Hawaii with his family.

Cashman asked Joe, *Is it true what the writers are saying?*

Torre said, simply, *No.*

9

HAL STEINBRENNER: THE ANTI-BOSS

Every team kicks off its season in April with a full tank of gas in the car. But energy derives from hope, and hope derives from wins; by July, you can often tell the winners from the losers by how they take the field between innings. If players still jog to their positions with purpose, they're probably running ahead in their division (or close behind) and expecting resupplies at the trade deadline. Watch them in the dugout when their team is up. Do they track at-bats and the pitcher's move to home, or do they sit there with their arms splayed across the bench, idly chatting up the guys beside them? Those are easy checks for a fan to perform; writers have other ways to read the meter. How many players are at their lockers before games, not hiding in their lounge or the video room? Are the monitors in the clubhouse tuned to other games, and if so, are the players watching with real interest?

But the surest tell of a team's direction is its manager's body language. For four and a half months, Boone sat up straight and met your gaze while taking questions. Accompanied by media relations director Jason Zillo, Boone whistled or hum-sang as he strode from his office to the pregame press conference. He then set up shop behind the batting cage, chanting encouragement to his guys. But bit by bit, the lassitude and losses of August set in, and by September Boone looked wrung dry.

On the West Coast road trip that began the final month, he plopped down in the press room after a loss to Oakland looking as pale as he had in March. The circles under his eyes had gathered mass, and for the first time you really felt him *wearing* these games at three or four in the morning. That was the night Severino was shelled for four runs before he broke a sweat in the first. Everything he threw got barreled up by the A's, just rope after rope to the gaps. Compounding his nightmare was Sánchez's performance: two passed balls and two wild pitches, all in one ungodly half-inning. The passed balls, by the way, were on heaters, not sliders. How on earth does a major league catcher muff a couple of *fastballs*?

It was as inexcusable as it was inexplicable, considering that Sánchez and Severino had been battery-mates since their late teens. "I have to do a better job than that," said Sánchez, but this latest mea culpa was roundly ignored. He'd been blowing the same smoke for a year and a half, and all he ever got was worse. In just fifty-nine games, he led the majors in passed balls and was costing his starters wins behind the plate. Boone barely touched on the matter after the loss, leaving it to his predecessor, Joe Girardi, to explain what the problem was. An analyst on MLB Network these days, Girardi went strong to the rack on Sánchez, rattling the rim with his comments. "His left knee collapses and he's not in position to catch and block some of these balls. You gotta fix that base," he said on national TV. "Until it's fixed, he's going to struggle."

But back to Boone, who bore the weight of those mistakes and seemed powerless to either fix or address them. After a game in Seattle that weekend, Boone went somewhere he hadn't gone before: he used the team's injuries as a shield. "Look how beat up we are," he groaned. "People say, 'I know you're missing so-and-so here and fill-in-the-blank there, but . . .' No: that's the *point*. We *are* missing those guys, and it really makes a difference for us."

He paused, took a breath to register what he'd said, then quickly tried to reel it back in. "Look, I walk through that clubhouse every day, and I know what we're made of here. We're going to be fine when we get some guys back. We're still a beast, and we know it."

It wasn't clear whom he hoped to convince. The division had slipped away, the A's were closing fast, and some lever seemed to have been thrown in Boone. For two-thirds of the season, he thought he had a handle on who his Yankees were. They were the Legion of Boom for opposing pitchers, a cast of heavy hitters with comic-book strength and more swag than a Drake-and-Yeezy tour. Only now they scared no one, not even the Twins, to whom they'd drop a series six days later. It's a terrible feeling to be running a team in September and have no idea what its nature is. Were these Yanks the same bullies who'd prevailed over the Astros, Sawx, and Indians in the first three months of the season? Or were they clueless meatheads whom the league had figured out and who were now presenting as a wild-card loser? Anyone claiming to know the answer to that question was lying through their teeth, and Boone wouldn't go there. Like everyone involved, he'd have to wait and see. But that's baseball, as someone — oh, yes, Boone himself — has said. It'll break your heart in half every time.

Back at the Stadium, the beatings continued, and morale did not improve. The Yanks dropped two of three to the fourth-place Blue Jays, who were clearly phoning the month in. Their manager, John Gibbons, had let it be known that he'd be stepping down at season's end. Meantime, he put across a lineup in the Bronx of not-yets and never-will-bes, including a starter in the middle game whose ERA neared seven. So naturally, that starter, Sean Reid-Foley, stonewalled the Yanks for five innings, departing with ten Ks and a shutout going. The story of the day, though, was CC Sabathia, who seemed to have finally run out of magic. As was first the case in Boston and then in Oakland, CC was blown out early. It was painful to watch the proud Samurai battle with nothing left in his scabbard. His cutter was suddenly a cookie that crumbled in the zone, dawdling up there at 87, not 90. A nonentity named Randal Grichuk crushed him for two homers, and the Blue Jays ran him out of there in the third. If you were looking for a marker on where the season was trending, here was as good a gloss as any. Till August, the Yanks had been counting on CC to pitch meaningful postseason innings. He'd been money in the 2017 playoffs, particularly the championship series, and a guy they'd leaned on heavily after losses. But in the course of the long summer, Sabathia's knee had worn down and he was essentially left naked out there. He wasn't ready to admit it — "I just have to make better pitches," he reflected, after the Blue Jays' shellacking — but minus his cutter, he couldn't command the corners with just a changeup and a lazy two-seamer.

There's a short list of great ones who knew they were done before life came knocking with the news. Jim Brown and Barry Sanders, Sandy Koufax and Mike Mussina, Björn Borg and Eric Cantona spring to mind. Somewhat more common are the legends who thrashed against the dying of the light. Michael Jordan and Johnny Unitas, Muhammad Ali and Jimmy Connors — none of them did their legacy any favors by squeezing out an extra couple of comebacks. The vast majority of legends learn the truth like most of us do: through a succession of pummeling blows. Their used-to-be homers now die before the wall, or their once-filthy cutter goes out for long rides and exits with a very loud bang.

So it was for CC, the seventh-inning sure thing who now couldn't muddle through the third. If his fall hurt more to witness than the aging of Brett Gardner, well, that's because it was *supposed* to hurt more. Both are fine men, both played their hearts out, and both did their fans and teammates honor. But CC, when great, was very nearly immortal and may have been the last of his kind. After he, and perhaps Verlander, have thrown their final heater, who will ever again get close to 250 wins and 3,000 strikeouts in a career? (Please, don't even mention 300 wins. That mark might as well be Mars now.) Who, in this age of gas-blasters and launch angles, will ever last long enough to pitch 3,500 innings and make 530-plus starts? If the Tampa Bays, Oaklands, and Milwaukees have their way, we may be chasing daylight on the traditional ace, the horse who eats 230 innings a year and pitches deep enough to approach twenty wins. Perhaps the game is headed toward a handful of guys who'll endure as unicorn starters — the Blake Snells and Gerrit Coles whom teams can count on thirty times to give them six or seven innings — while filling in around them with long men and bridge guys and short-term loaners from Triple-A. We're not there yet, thank God, and accursed be the day when the word "opener" replaces "starter" in our syntax.

Alas, the Yanks' pitching staff, like their lineup, was on fumes, and they had no choice but to ride Sabathia through season's end. Severino was all over the map in his starts, getting blasted by the A's, losing a messy one to the Twins, then dominating the Red Sox at home. From outing to outing, no one had a fix on which Severino would show up: the free-and-easy ace with the disappearing fastball who'd been the best pitcher in baseball for three months, or the confused and flustered kid who'd lose the feel for both his pitches and couldn't course-correct on the mound. "You just have to keep in mind how young he is, and that these fluctuations are normal at his stage," Cashman noted. "Because he's so talented, his sine curve goes straight up *and* straight down. For us, it's a matter of riding out his slumps."

But because Severino had been such a cipher in the second half — fourteen starts, a 6-6 record, and an ERA in the mid-sixes — he'd jacked up the stakes on his fellow starters. Sonny Gray was serving out his exile in the pen, from whence he'd make occasional cameos in blowout wins and losses. The Lance Lynn experiment had proved a wash: four solid starts mixed in with four stinkers and a couple of five-and-flys. At thirty-one, he was long past his frontline days and would most likely be pitching for someone else come the spring. And CC, for all his first-half heroics, had nine wins to show for his apparent swan-song season. That left the Yanks with two defensible options to start the wild-card game against Oakland: Masahiro Tanaka and J. A. Happ.

Both had pitched superbly for the bulk of their season, though Happ, of course, began his in Toronto. As a Yankee, he'd been the second coming of Jimmy Key: a master practitioner of hitting his spots and never giving an inch with runners on. (His regular-season numbers with the Yanks: eleven starts, a 7-0 record, and an ERA of 2.69.) Granted, won-loss records have shrunk in value: Jacob deGrom would earn the Cy Young Award with the lowest win total ever for a starting pitcher. Still, Happ's seventeen wins in '18 were a fair reflection of his worth. He never had wipeout stuff as a kid, and now, at thirty-six, he had just enough life on his four-seam fastball to keep it off the barrel of the bat. Happ, too, is something of a vanishing breed: the tai chi wizard who wins by deception and by keeping fastball hitters off balance. He throws his hard stuff about 75 percent of the time, a remarkably high use rate at any age, and averages a velocity of 92, which scares no one in these days of 101. But it's the illusionist things he does with his 92 that makes him so uncomfortable to face.

First, he commands the four quadrants of the plate — down and in, up and away, etc. — so he's constantly changing eye level for a hitter. Second, he adds and subtracts a couple of miles, inducing weak swings and late decisions. Third, he throws his heater with so much spin that it gains *perceived velocity* at the plate. Several Red Sox and Yanks spoke about Happ's fastball, all giving variants of the same answer: "The scoreboard gun might say 92, but it looks more like 96 when you're in the box," said Andrew Benintendi, the stellar Red Sox left fielder.

"His fastball plays up big time." Mookie Betts and Aaron Judge said the pitch seems to rise, or in hitters' parlance, "take off." "It's a gift, man," said Betts, the year's runaway MVP. "He keeps the ball up in the hitting zone, and it never comes down." Said Judge, who struck out six of the ten times he faced Happ when Happ was with the Jays: "It looks like it's coming in belt-high, and I'd think, *I got this*, and swing, then be like, *How'd I miss that pitch?*" Stanton gave a more concise assessment: "He messes with your depth perception."

Hitting is all about timing and balance, which is why major leaguers *crush* pitching machines when they step into the cage. You can set that bad boy at 100 if you want: when a hitter knows what's coming and from which angle it will issue, he can gin up his hand speed to pound it. But Happ, like Greg Maddux and many virtuosi before him, constantly spoils their stride by throwing gas at different speeds and pitching to different spots. Those high pitch counts he always seems to run, which reduce him to a six-inning pitcher? He gets foul ball after foul ball on emergency hacks as guys barely make contact to stay alive. Fun fact: Happ had the sixth-highest foul ball/foul tip percentage (22 percent) in MLB, just behind Verlander, Cole, and Scherzer in 2018. Generally, the hardest throwers get the most late swings. That Happ is on that list is a testament to his skill — and a beacon of hope to lesser arms.

Happ, as mild a man as you're ever going to meet in the setting of a major league clubhouse, has the demeanor of an FM deejay. He's tall and bald and bewildered to hear his praises sung, particularly from the mouths of superstars. "Believe me, I'm not perfect," he says. "I've made my share of mistakes."

And learned from them it seems. As a young pitcher, he'd get enraged at himself each time he threw a bad inning. "I was the kind of guy who thought he should never make a mistake," he says, and the hitters could always tell. They would take more pitches and make him work harder, then watch him unravel in games. Finally, approaching thirty, he looked in the mirror and decided to change things. "I wasn't going to give them a competitive edge by letting them see me that way."

On the mound, he affected a robotic calm that eventually worked down deep below the skin. Now it's second nature — and contagious. The Yanks seem much more relaxed behind him, less prone to jumpy plays and bad at-bats. Indeed, the only doubter since his arrival was Happ himself: the day he joined the team, he looked around the clubhouse and realized he knew no one in the room. "There's a certain stress level after a trade — you're trying to prove they made a good decision," says Happ, who's been traded five times. Then he went out and won five straight games before taking a no-decision against the Tigers. "The most important pick-up of our season," Boone says. "We wouldn't be where we are without J.A."

Tanaka, who threw 97 when the Yankees first signed him as a widely sought free agent in 2014, has evolved and adapted from his days of thunder in the Nippon Professional League. (He once won twenty-five decisions in a row there, the most by a pitcher in any professional league, including MLB.) He was largely untouchable in his rookie season with the Yanks, starting 11-1 and making the All-Star team before partially tearing a ligament in his pitching arm just before the break. (Almost exactly the same thing happened to Shohei Ohtani in his debut season with the Angels. It is a dicey proposition for men who throw as hard as they do to come to America from Japan. There, they make only one start a week and a couple of dozen, total, for the year. Here, of course, it's every five days and three dozen starts, playoffs included.)

But Tanaka, a man of honor who happens to play baseball, chose rest and rehab over Tommy John surgery, which would have cost the Yanks his services for eighteen months. After a handful of starts at the end of 2014, Tanaka returned for good in 2015 and was, perforce, a transformed pitcher: he had to live now on his wits and precision. He throws

basically two pitches: a slider that dives late and low to left-handed hitters, and a knee-high fastball that drops off the table a foot or so from
the plate. That pitch is Tanaka's notorious splitter, and when he's throwing it for strikes — or almost-strikes — it's nearly impossible to put the
bat-head on it. It doesn't just dive — it darts at the ankles of a hitter in
the right-handed box. To be sure, he has a third pitch, but it's just for
show: a high four-seamer to keep the hitters honest.

Roughly three out of every four starts he makes, Tanaka is Tanaka,
a ghost-face killer. He throws everything just below the hollow of the
knee and gets a lot of weak contact and queasy at-bats. But then there's
that fourth start, where he can't command the splitter and leaves it up
around the thigh to get thrashed. (The joke in the press box among the
beat writers is that the fourth game is ordered by the Yakuza, Japan's
organized crime syndicates, who make a fortune betting on his losses.)

The problem for the Yankees, and presumably Tanaka as well, is that
they never know when that fourth start is coming. He'll pitch superbly
against the Indians, Angels, and Mariners, then get the stuffing beaten
out of him by the Orioles. Nor could they know what Tanaka would
give them come October, since they'd made exactly one playoff run in
the four prior years they'd had him. He'd been terrific in the three starts
he'd made in '17 (2-1, twenty innings, and a 0.90 ERA), but none of
those outings were in Fenway. There, he'd been fair to solid till 2018,
when the Red Sox either lit him up or waited him out. No, their best
option against Boston was Happ (lifetime: 7-4, 2.83 ERA), so they'd
have to roll the dice on Sevy in the wild card and hope he'd pitch them
through to the divisional round.

In the meantime, the Yankees needed to beat someone — *anyone* — just
to hang on to home-field against Oakland. They'd begun September by
losing eight of fourteen and barely hitting a lick in most of those games.
After a particularly galling 3–2 loss to the Jays — they'd somehow been

four-hit over seven innings by a kid named Tom Pannone — the question was put to Cashman: "What's happened to your team? You had a *great* trade deadline: guessed right on Happ and Voit and Britton and McCutchen. So how do you try and understand this?"

Cashman has essentially two expressions: an upturned brow with a *very* slight grin when he's amused by something you said, and — the other 98 percent of the time — the scrunched lips and fixed stare of someone hunched over a bomb, trying to guess which wire must be cut. "You're right," he said, "we got a bunch of good players, which is why I'm scratching my head now." He paused, presumably *not* to scratch his head, then turned to a trope he'd used before. "We're really missing Judge," he said. "Not just his bat but his presence."

Here, in one sentence, was the team's self-diagnosis of what befell it in the second half of the season. What Cash meant by Judge's *presence* was a panoply of things: his patience at the plate and the way it filtered down to the guys hitting behind him in the order; his energy in the dugout, which can't be overvalued in a squad that lacks a fireball for a skipper; and his authority in the clubhouse among the younger guys, on whom the Yanks had come so dearly to depend. But above all, Cash meant that squishiest thing of all: a team's core sense of who it is. *With* Judge, the Yankees are a very good team that firmly believes it is great. Without him, they are something more diffuse and less effective: a collection of very good players. Judge — like Jeter and the great Yanks before them — is the spiritual compound that binds his squad together and embodies its truest essence — *when he plays.*

That last clause is crucial, because his powers diminish in direct proportion to his presence. As Judge himself said during his two-month absence, his lack of impact "just kills me." He couldn't "get into guys" about their level of play when he was "sitting on the bench wearing a hoodie." He couldn't "tell 'em '*LET'S GO!*'" when he was on the DL and reduced to "just watching and chewing gum." Then there was his disappearance *off* the field. Like Jeter was for Torre (at least in his prime), Judge is his manager's first lieutenant. Torre never had to go police his clubhouse; Jeter did that for him for ten years. All it took was a look or a throat-clear from Jetes and Nick Johnson and Ricky Ledée snapped to attention.

So it is with Judge, who quietly cracks the whip when the cohort of Miggy and Gleyber gets sloppy. Boone's specialty isn't tough love, it's consensus-building, so someone has to lean in for him. That's what Judge does the second he suits up: he hardens his team's resolve and dedication. It shouldn't be that way, but it is *always* that way, at least on teams that are going places. When Judge walks into the room and suits up for a game, everyone's heart beats quicker. You can't put a price or a WAR tag on that. You just have to see it to know its worth.

Meanwhile, somewhere in the folds of Yankee Stadium, one man sat calmly at his desk, watching the seesaw season play out. Hal Steinbrenner isn't an executive given to wild mood swings; he is every inch the cut of a contemporary chairman. He shows up for an interview in a pale-colored pullover and a pair of well-pressed khakis (is the *entire* Yankees staff sponsored by Ralph Lauren?) and has the bearing of a guy you've met for drinks after a gratifying round of golf. In tone and in gesture, he is made to measure for the culture of a modern corporation. He is handsome in a tousled, uncreased way and has a gentleness about him that is almost jarring, given his shrill genetics. You can hear George in his voice, but only faintly: it is there as a trace element and nothing more. Where his father talked intently, as if his words were under pressure, Hal speaks strictly in an indoor pitch that is somehow both relaxed and conserved. It isn't a thing he's practiced and gotten better at over the years. It is rather a manifesting of who he is: the prudent son of an imprudent father who resolved, at an early age, to be different.

That is explicitly who he's become: the hyperefficient, if reticent, successor to one of the most charismatic owners in sports history. Hal did not in any way want the job or ask for it. There was something he liked better: the hotel trade. "I had my own group that I put together," he begins, sitting in the office of his sister Jennifer. "We owned a couple of hotels in Sarasota and one in Jacksonville, and I oversaw George's hotels in Ocala. I just loved everything about that business — finding a piece of dirt, convincing bankers this was a good place to build a building, then building the building and running it."

But the team, and his obligation to it, kept calling, even before George took ill. "I had spent a lot of years in the [Tampa office] getting pulled into meetings with him, and I suddenly realized that this is not a job I've been in tune with for at least five years." He'd always savored living in Florida, where he went home to his wife and kids at day's end, instead of keeping a suite in mid-Manhattan. And he was "frankly intimidated by the team business, which had grown quite a lot while I was down there." But as George declined and his succession plans shifted (the intent had been to hand the team to his son-in-law, Steve Swindal, until Steve's divorce from Jenny Steinbrenner), Hal bowed to the wishes of his parents and siblings and stepped up in the mid-2000s. Despite his distance from it, the CEO role wasn't a reach: "This was always in my blood — I grew up with this team. It was just trying to figure out, how will this go?"

Whether George meant to or not — and one can probably assume he didn't — his youngest son shares both a name and a disposition with another famous prince: Hal, the ambivalent son of Henry the Fourth. The focal point of one of William Shakespeare's greatest plays, Prince Hal would, of course, become Henry the Fifth and miraculously defeat the French at Agincourt — but he too was yanked, if not kicking and screaming, to his predestined place on the throne. It bears noting that *George's* Hal didn't spend his pregame years carousing with the likes of

Falstaff and Bardolph. Still, being placed atop the masthead of the New York Yankees needed some getting used to, and some time.

"There was a transition that . . . took a couple of years" is all he ventures on that head before shifting adroitly to other matters. In leadership, he acknowledges, he isn't at all like his father, whom he refers to as "a micromanager." "I hire and hold on to competent people so that they can make decisions that don't involve me," he says, adding that most of his executives "have been here twenty-plus years and take a tremendous amount of pride" in that. Hal's job entails being the final decider on each of the key initiatives that Cashman brings him. On other teams, Cashman would probably be making those calls and "have a hell of a lot more ability to do the things he wanted without the owner being involved." Still, Hal says, "90 percent of what Cash wants gets done because I trust him and his people. They know a lot more about this stuff than I do." In the end, though, "those decisions are *financial* decisions that affect the capability of this team."

And there we quickly are, on Topic A: the team's payroll and his mission to pare it. Hal leaps at the chance to explain his thinking, speaking in yards, not inches. "It's just logical that you shouldn't have to have a $250 million payroll to compete for a pennant," he says. "Now, we struggled for years, because our development system was lacking and we had nobody to come up and help out. My dad tended, as you know, to trade away good young people to win now, now, now, now, now. I can't tell you how many times, over the last five years, teams asked us for Judge and Sánchez and Severino and others, and year after year we refused. So now here we are, with all these young stars that we can promote to our fans on social media and a system where everybody still wants our minor leaguers now that these guys have come up. I don't take credit for much, but I *will* take credit for that, and Cash was right on board with me."

He tacks to the subject of those prospects and their fans. "I think baseball has had a problem with millennials, and we, in the past, have had that too. Have you ever been to an NYCFC soccer game here? There's a *lot* of millennials there. It's two hours, in and out, and the action's nonstop, except for the halftime break. We recognized that three years ago — that even millennial viewers on YES were down — and that we needed to address this problem. We met with advertising agencies that specialize in this generation and learned a lot from them. It became clear that millennials wanted to watch baseball standing up, with a beer in their hand, talking to their friends while Instagramming and Snapchatting."

Hal, an R-and-D geek, was now in his sweet spot: the harmonic convergence of knowledge and opportunity. "What we immediately did — it's a $20 million investment, but one that was a no-brainer to me — was to go ahead and build gathering spots in the outfield decks, on either side of the batter's eye. It's really three different areas, and anybody can go out there, it's not a club you [have to pay to get into]. What we're finding is that it's packed from beginning of game to end, and there are people of all ages out there. They're Snapchatting and Instagramming, and it's a great place to watch a game. Other clubs have done it now, the same type of concept. This is the second year we've had the decks."

We note that his attendance is up again this year, by about 330,000 fans, and that the team has jumped from sixth to second in MLB's box-office ranks.

"Well, what's up is *millennial* attendance," he notes, almost, but not quite, boasting. "Because of all the efforts we've made in social media, starting a department and hiring people to focus on this full-time, YES's viewership in millennials is up too. That's because they're getting to know these young players, and the one thing I insisted on is that we have in-game spots for highlights of our minor league players. Get to know [Estevan] Florial, [Justus] Sheffield, they're up and coming, and we did *The Road to the Show* [a reality TV series] on YES. We're doing live Twitter with the players being interviewed by fans, and the millennials are excited about them and about what we've done to the stadium. It makes the *experience* for them more than just the game and what's going on on the field."

He could go on in the experiential vein, but the Red Sox are in town, game time is nearing, and there's an important line of inquiry left. When you get the most privacy-minded owner in baseball in front of you, you don't want to waste the chance to empty your notebook.

"I have to ask this," says Klapisch, who began covering the team in the mid-'80s after graduating from Columbia. "My first job at the *Post* was to call George every day and wait by the phone for his callback. This was back before Steinbrenner Field or Yankee headquarters in Tampa, so I'd have to call American Shipbuilding in those days. Then the phone would ring [with his callback], and he would just start *talking,* wouldn't even say it was George. And I've gotta say, your dad scared the hell out of me —"

"You? He scared the hell out of *all of us!*" Hal puts in, and the four grown men around the table, Zillo included, roar with laughter — and relief.

"So, I'm just wondering . . . what is it like for you to follow in those footsteps?" Klapisch continues. "You're clearly not the person who wants to dominate New York, be the talk of the town. You don't intimidate people, it's not how you're wired, and I'm curious what was it like to grow up with that, and to follow in those footsteps professionally?"

Hal gives a laugh, as if to forewarn us that he won't be diving deeply in *those* waters. "Yeah, look, growing up was tough, with what the kids said [to me] at school and him always [being] in the papers. Those weren't easy years, there were some lousy teams, and also, our personalities are *completely* different. He was a coach. I wasn't. He was a good athlete. I wasn't. I'm an introvert. I love walking in the park for two hours and having no one recognize me. A few months ago, I ran into Billy Crystal there, and he had the hat on, the glasses, the beard. I thought, *What an awful way to live.* I can't imagine it. It's not my persona, and I don't want that for my kids."

"So, at no time in these last two months have you been tempted to call the *Post* and yell, 'Stanton's hitting .240 since the break!'"

Hal laughs again, a surprised little chuckle that's like a lull in the regatta. "No. I have the greatest appreciation for your profession, and I hope you know that, but I'm not going to use the newspapers to accomplish something. I'm going to try to accomplish it in-house."

"And you're telling us you never hear George whisper in your ear, 'Go *get* those so-and-sos who aren't hitting'?"

"Actually, I get that from my *mom*," he chortles. "No shit. She's eighty-three, and she's like, 'You need to go down to that clubhouse and start yelling at them!' And I'm like, '*Mom!* You say that all the time!'"

"And *did* you go down there?"

"No, I don't do that. It's not my personality, and I'm not convinced it's effective. And yet somehow, they find a way to turn it around. Last year they went to Game 7 of the ALCS."

"I ask that because George *loved* going down there — it was part of who he was," Klapisch prods. "Do you love what you're doing? Love it the way he loved it?"

Hal lets out a breath before answering. "Look, clearly, *he* loved it, it was his passion. Me? I find it . . . challenging. Yes, it's a lot of fun, but a lot of tough times too, being in a family business. It's a blessing, but also an added challenge that maybe other CEOs don't have. Look, I wouldn't be doing this if my name wasn't Steinbrenner — I recognize and appreciate that. So I try to treat the job with respect, because I don't deserve to be here, that's just a fact. If my name wasn't Steinbrenner, I *wouldn't* be here."

We're startled to hear that: he wears the crown jewels now like one to the manor born. But it's almost first pitch for Severino versus Price, and everyone is glancing at his watch. So one last query is put to him: "We know how many times George almost sold the team. Have you ever considered selling it yourself?"

Hal, the careful, self-disclaiming owner, pounces on the question like a hare. "Never," he says flatly. "I've never considered it. We're not selling and getting out."

And there, for just a moment, flits the old man's ghost in the timbre of his son's voice.

That Shakespeare fellow: boy, did he know power. He would've been one hell of a Yankee fan.

10

NUMBER 99: HELLO, BOYS, I'M BAAACK!

At some point in the afternoon of September 14, word went out on all the arms of social media: Aaron Judge had been activated by the New York Yankees for their game against Toronto that evening. It was a Friday night affair, so the place would be good and jacked with that end-of-the-week jolt the city supplies. Though the transit authorities that service the Stadium explicitly ban beer-drinking on board, virtually every train that stops there on home-game Fridays is a block party of brown paper bags. Even some of the women wearing Aaron Judge jerseys pour out of the cars bellowing *BOSTON SUCKS!* So many cops in riot gear await you on the platform, you'd think you'd stumbled into some drunken conflation of St. Patty's Day and SantaCon. But no, you're in the Bronx, and it's just another baseball weekend — and don't be caught uptown in Blue Jays blue.

This night, however, was different from all the others, and *not* because Yom Kippur was around the corner. Fans had come out early to get a glimpse of Their Lord and Savior, packing the outfield stands at 5:00 p.m. Alas, Judge didn't come out for late BP, so they'd have to wait till game time for their fix. For eight weeks, the Stadium had been strangely mute, lacking its usual noise and nastiness. In Judge's absence, the team had played average ball, and average baseball is dull — and death to ambience. Whatever else happened tonight, this crowd would be on *tilt*. All it needed was an on-field sighting of Judge to explode.

In the clubhouse before the game, the room was electric and loud. Every player was at his locker, talking mess to the guys next to him. It felt like a *football* game was about to break out. Judge himself had been on edge all day, sprinting in the outfield, taking early BP, and just generally being a pain in the ass to Boone. "I've been voicing my opinion around here — a *lot*," he confided to Klapisch, meaning he'd been lobbying his manager hard to return. Judge had hoped to see his name on the lineup card that night, but Boone wasn't ready to write him in. The trainers were still erring on the side of caution, giving Judge a few more days before facing in-game pitching. Still, he started heating up in the tunnel, getting a sweat going by the third inning. Then the Yanks jumped out to a 9–0 lead, and every eye in the park was on their dugout.

In the top of the eighth, the crowd's patience was rewarded. The moment Judge got one of his cleats up on the cinders, the ballpark erupted. It takes a lot of hopping to make the new joint jump. It's much stouter and better buttressed than the previous building, which sometimes swayed like a bridge in high winds. As Judge ran out to his spot in right field as a defensive replacement for Andrew McCutchen, the concrete underfoot pulsed and shook. Cutch, who'd been moved over to left by Boone, purposely lagged behind in the dugout to gauge the crowd's reaction. "Unbelievable," he said at his locker after the game. "I had no idea how much he meant here till I saw it happen. That was pretty impressive, man. Shows you what kind of leader that dude is."

McCutchen, a very old soul for thirty-one, has been a leader, and a dude, of the first rank. The five-time All-Star and former National League MVP, he was the franchise player in Pittsburgh for nine seasons before being dealt to the Giants. Now a quiet, watchful vet content to be in the chorus, he'd been enjoying his change of fortune since the Yanks acquired him in August. Each day for the previous week, he'd staked his spot behind the cage to watch Judge and Stanton take their rips. What he saw made him hang his jaw in amazement—and regret that he hadn't been around for the full season. "To people who've been here all year, I guess that [BP] stuff is normal. Trust me, it's *not* normal. You don't hit balls that far." He said it was a privilege to be on this team, and the feeling was clearly mutual. Cashman was already tinkering with the idea of re-signing McCutchen before free agency would commence in November.

Judge got only two innings in right that night. Boone acknowledged after the game that if the Yanks had batted around, he would have pulled him rather than let him swing the bat. It took four more days, and a simulated game, for Judge to finally convince his skipper he was good to go. On September 18, a Tuesday, the Red Sox came to town, and there, on the lineup card posted outside the clubhouse, was Judge in his usual two-hole. *That* night the park was an adrenaline zoo, thrumming with pent-up energy—and fury. Nearly fifty thousand people showed up to the Stadium. Very few of them were school-age children.

There are certain nights (and opponents) when almost every attendee knows it's not wise to bring the kids. If they come, they're going to watch grown men model behaviors that, once seen, can't easily be unseen. They're also going to witness something relatively new here: a fully weaponized fan base. At the old Yankee Stadium, the grandstands jutted out like the overbite of a very big shark. Opposing outfielders feared for their lives, and for good reason. In the past, folks in the bleachers threw beer cans and coins at them and rained down awful calumnies about the sex lives of their mothers. Then the new park went up, with its sveltely recessed stands and aggressively priced ticket-package plans, and so many of those beer-lunged welders and firefighters stayed home to watch the games on YES. For years they were replaced by the Vineyard Vines set, perfectly fine people from perfectly fine towns in Westchester and lower Connecticut. But the folks in blue blazers didn't bring the same *hatred* that the goons in camo hats did, and the so-called stars the Yankees were fielding then (Jacoby Ellsbury, Carlos Beltrán, Brian McCann, et al.) didn't evoke the same passions — or any passion at all, to be precise.

Then the Baby Bombers arrived, and Hal Steinbrenner opened up those beer gardens in left and right field and — well, you don't see a lot of guys in checked shirts and oxfords communing in the bleachers anymore. If those former frat boys are still attending in numbers, they've adopted the mufti of the working stiff: a team-licensed ball cap, a pair of cargo jeans, and either a replica jersey or a snarky T-shirt with a Yankee spin. In the bottom of the first, Judge walked to the plate for his first at-bat in two months. No description of the ovation is needed here, save to say it was long and loud. Nate Eovaldi, the ex-Yankee he was facing that night, can be a very tall order these days. Two years after his second Tommy John surgery, which submarined his New York tenure, he was back throwing 100 with a two-seam tilt, an equally filthy splitter, and an inhuman cutter he'd added that lit up the radar gun at 91. Eovaldi's previous start against the Yankees was game 3 of the sweep in Fenway, when he'd badly overmatched the Bombers for eight shutout innings, allowing three hits and a walk. But on this night Judge stood in there like he hadn't missed a moment and belted a 112-mile-an-hour rocket. Unfortunately, he hit it directly at J. D. Martinez. Five feet over in either direction, it would have gouged the wall in right for a double.

His second at-bat, Judge scorched another cutter, this one to Bogaerts at short. Happy just to get his glove up in time, Bogaerts snared it and adroitly turned two. In his third AB, Judge was unluckier still: he just missed hitting a two-run homer when Martinez chased his drive down on the track. After striking out in the eighth, Judge took an oh-for-four collar and had to settle for some moral satisfaction.

But the Yankees won the game that night, and the next night too, and then went on a vicious tear the last two weeks of the season. It is impossible to overstate the obvious with Judge: he *is* the New York Yankees, full stop, period. Didi and Sánchez had been back for weeks, the bullpen had filled in capably for Chapman, but the team was sub-.500 in September until their leader returned. Judge himself was circumspect about his impact: it hurt him still to swing, he confided privately, and you could see that pain reflected in his numbers. In the twelve games he started before the wild-card round, he hit .220 with just a single home run and several drives that died before the track. Part of that shortfall was due to timing: he was *just* a hair off with some swings, barely missing the barrel on crushable pitches. And part of it was human: it would have hurt him beyond measure if he aggravated the wrist and missed the playoffs.

But his effect on the team's morale, and on the players hitting behind him, was unmistakable: "He makes us feel better, especially us young guys," said Gleyber Torres, who then added, sotto voce, "he's like our captain." "Just his *presence* is uplifting, and you don't see that in young players," noted Neil Walker. "He gets everyone in the lineup easier at-bats because they're back hitting in spots where they belong." "He commands your respect just by walking in the clubhouse," said Austin Romine, the eagle-eyed catcher. "A player of that caliber who eats and sleeps baseball — hell, he makes you love it too."

And suddenly, the somnolent New York offense was awake, terrorizing pitchers again. Those last two weeks, the Yanks bashed homer after homer, easily breaking the major league mark of 264 in a season. They overwhelmed the teams left on their schedule, including two series with the Red Sox and a four-gamer down in Tampa, which had been the Yanks' House of Horrors all year. Here, at long last, was the club we'd seen in June: the Wheel of Death lineup that never seemed to end, with assassin after assassin in a row. Except now it was even longer and more power-packed: they'd added another bruiser in Luke Voit, the strapping kid Cashman pickpocketed from the Cardinals at the trading deadline.

Since joining the Yanks in August — a month when he played spar-ingly and was actually sent down to the minors for a bit — Voit had sud-denly channeled the Jason Giambi who'd won an MVP trophy with the A's. *That* Jason Giambi — whom the Yankees barely saw after George signed him to a massive contract after the '01 season — was impossible to pitch to for his last four years in Oakland. He hit line to line with power, drew staggering numbers of walks, and struck out very rarely for a bodybuilder who bashed forty homers a year. So too with Voit, who had languished for several years in the Cardinals' organization. A middle linebacker in high school and a devoted power-lifter built like a slightly shorter and leaner Roger Clemens, he'd bogged himself down by bringing a gladiator's fury to the task of hitting a curveball. "I lost my temper a lot," Voit says of his five-year quest for a proper mind-set in the minors. "It took me a long time to realize that baseball's 90 percent mental and that brute strength alone will end your career."

Twenty-seven now, he's a sweet, funny man-child who comes across like a goofy personal trainer. He packs the sort of short-strand, bunched-up mass you rarely see these days in double-knits — but on Voit, that muscle is pneumatic. His bat is quick to the ball, adjusts for late breaks, and covers the whole zone at the plate. Since he learned to harness his rage — a development for which he credits his fiancée, Tori Rigman, whom he planned to marry over the winter — the kid who'd hit five homers *total* in parts of two seasons with St. Louis had become a wrecking ball with the Yanks. In little more than a month since the club recalled him from its Triple-A team in Scranton, he'd hit fourteen homers, driven in better than a run a game, and posted an OPS of 1.069, which is Mookie Betts/Mike Trout good. More, he'd brought a kind of little kid's glee into the batter's box. Every time he got hold of a hanger, he hop-skipped his first step toward first base, the sort of thing you see in youth travel ball.

By September, Voit had wrested first base from Bird, though his glove was, to put this kindly, ornamental. He was erratic when tossing to second to force the lead runner, and every short-hopped throw to first was heart-in-throat exciting, especially when that throw came from Miggy. Defensively, the Yanks' corner guys were *Dracula Versus Wolfman,* a low-rent monster movie from the 1940s. But that too was part of the bargain Cashman had made when he went whole hog on power over the winter. His team wasn't going to beat you with defense and speed and the sentimental pleasures of hit-and-run baseball. No, from one to nine now, it was one long truncheon, a blunt instrument to wield at opposing starters. If you were Blake Snell–precise, you could use their aggression against them, sucker them into chasing off the corners. (Snell proved that point in two-hitting the Yankees over five innings in August, striking out six while barely breaking a sweat.) Short of that, though, you either had Verlander's riding fastball or you were in for a nasty, brutish night — particularly if the game was in the Bronx.

Because something else happened over those last two weeks that didn't show up in the line scores. This team and this town fell wildly back in love, and the yield of that passion was a beast. It was noise and turbulence and a charge in the air that took hold of you before you passed through the gate. You felt it walking up there or on the train ride over, a mob convergence of tension and mass: the tribe marching off to battle. If you're a baseball fan reading this in St. Louis or San Diego, you will have no frame of reference for the sort of dark fervor that consumes a pennant crowd in the Northeast. Savage and joyous and fiercely profane, it's a buildup and expulsion of adrenalized pride that is easily mistaken for rage. You'll find it, in spades, at Fenway Park, and for decades it presented in the Yanks' previous stadium: the brute power of a crowd to disable opposing teams before they take the field.

In the fall of '17, the Astros suffocated the Yanks with powerhouse pitching in Houston. Then they came to the Bronx, up two games to none, and were utterly unmanned by the crowd. The Yanks crushed them three straight, outscored them 19–5, and held them to eleven hits *total*. The playoffs that year were a revival meeting — the raising of the dead park's ghosts. For the very first time in its nine-year run, the Stadium was a terror-dome. No accident, that. The fans finally had a team to go to war for — and vice versa, as things turned out.

Forget the wild-card club of 2015: it was pale and passive and consisted of creaky strangers who were paid a lot of money to pose as Yankees. But the Baby Bomber bunch who'd climbed the rungs together and come of age precipitously that summer in '17 — those were the *true* sons of New York. With their mackadocious blend of youth and muscle, they reflected handsomely on their fans — or their fans' most romantic self-conception. New Yorkers, *wherever* they're from, nurse the crazed conceit that they're bigger, smarter, and vastly better-looking than people in off-brand towns. There's a reason they stick around to hear Sinatra sing after *thuuhhhh Yankees win*. "New York, New York" expresses the sacrosanct myth that they — the team's followers — are themselves the "King of the hill / Top of the list / A number one." That the hill in question is a hill of hooey — this town doesn't make you bigger, and this ball club doesn't make you brighter — is entirely beside the point. What matters is the product of that mutual infatuation: a thing that people politely call *synergy*. Of course, in the Bronx, where no one calls *anything* politely, they know it by its right name: *COME AND GET YOUR ASS, MOTHERFUCKERS!*

Which brings us back to love, and its alchemical power to resonate as hate toward visiting teams. When the Oakland A's touched down in New York City to play the wild-card game, they had every reason to puff their chests — and to book a connecting flight to Boston. They were essentially the Yankees, just younger and cheaper, with the third-smallest payroll in the game. There was power up and down their hirsute

lineup, including the majors' home run king, Khris Davis. They had six
or seven guys coming out of the pen throwing 97 or better, among them
the hottest closer in baseball, Blake Treinen. They'd suffered and survived their own spate of cruel injuries, chiefly to their starting rotation.
Still, they'd been the planet's best team since June, winning sixty-three
of their last ninety-two. In short, they were even hotter than the Yanks.

"Nobody had us winning ninety-seven this year, but we were able
to wear teams out," said Billy Beane over the phone before the game.
"Even the best pitchers, we got them out of there by the sixth because
we drew so many walks and hit home runs." For a team "with the fewest
resources," they played "great infield defense and beat good teams on
the road. Also, our guys are too young to be afraid." Asked how they'd
reacted when the Yanks clinched home-field, Beane essentially yawned
at the question. "Oh, they're fine with it," he said. "They're like, 'We'll be
that much closer to Boston when we win.'"

And then the Athletics went out and stretched in front of a house that
was packed *three hours* before the ball game. Just getting to the park had
required running an armed gauntlet that jammed the roads for miles
in both directions. There were counterterror troops at the major inter-
sections, backed up by K-9 squads and precinct cops; the South Bronx
was a *quinceañera* of red and blue lights. Inside, on the concourse, lines
fanned out for beer; by the looks of it, most of the red-cheeked patrons
began pregaming right around lunch. There were roars every time a
couple of Yankees jogged out to long-toss on the track. When Judge
knelt down in the outfield grass to cross himself and pray, the crowd
took his cue and fell silent a moment, its first — and last — moment of
reverence. By the time they introduced the players of both teams up the
first- and third-base lines, the place was a shriek machine. Press-box
veterans remarked that this was the loudest the Stadium had been all
year. Rarely would they see its sound and fury crumple a pitcher completely.

The A's, as mentioned, had lost most of their starters to one serious injury or another, including their marvelous lefty Sean Manaea. They'd endured by signing several scrap-heap arms and adopting the Tampa trick of using openers. Liam Hendriks, a vagabond short man who'd found his calling, at twenty-nine, as a thirty-pitch-or-less starting pitcher, was a puddle of pudding on the mound. He walked McCutchen, the leadoff batter, on five shaky pitches, then fell behind the two-hitter, Judge. On his ninth pitch, a straight-as-a-string two-seamer, Judge fired his back hip, whipped the barrel of the bat through, and demolished the thigh-high fastball. It left his bat traveling 116 miles per hour and easily cleared the State Farm sign in left, a 427-foot *line drive* that was the hardest-hit homer in postseason history (or at least the part of history tracked by Statcast's lasers).

Both the ballpark and the Yankees' dugout went bonkers. For sixty or ninety seconds, everyone pogoed in place, wildly high-fiving the nearest stranger and howling like Samoan rugby players. Hendriks, the helpless waif, ignored the blast on contact, then turned at the last instant to watch it land. Exactly two hitters into the game, the Athletics were done, their spines and spirits broken beyond repair. (Said Fernando Rodney, the veteran A's reliever, after the game: "Once I saw how Judge hit that ball, I thought to myself, *This is over.*") Any false hopes they nursed were stubbed out in the sixth, when Judge led off with a double. Hicks promptly drove him home, then scored on a two-run triple by Voit, and from that point on the A's were just chew toys for the crowd. The park was still deafening in the bottom of the eighth when Stanton hit a homer a very far piece out to left. At 443 feet and a velo of 117.4, it snatched Judge's short-lived record away, though Judge — as is his wont — couldn't have cared less. He was both the game's conquering general and the homecoming king of the blowout party that started after the game.

. . .

These days, every clubhouse is set-dressed the same after a clinching win. The lockers, cubbies, and carpets are taped in plastic sheeting, and the players greet each other wearing expensive goggles and cheap-o commemorative caps. Reporters, at least the smart ones, come strapped with a poncho: the place is a cafeteria fight of barely drinkable bubbly. The joy was general and belligerent, with a couple of top notes layered on. One of them was giddy relief: the Yanks had been genuinely concerned about the A's, who'd beaten them up in Oakland one month prior. But in the shouted conversations going on in every corner, all the players were talking about the Sawx. From game 1, their season had been a hard-target chase of the Eternal Rival, a maddening hunt for a team that never slumped or dropped for a couple of weeks into lower gear. Twice, the Sox had opened up a sizable lead and been run down by the Yanks — when both teams were whole and healthy.

But then Sánchez got hurt, and Judge fell hard behind him, and the second half of the season became a survival course for the ball club in the Bronx. It somehow wasn't fair, in the sporting sense of that word: the Yanks had sent a skeleton squad to play that pivotal set in August. But now they had their leader back, their lineup of loaded cannons, and a prepacked building of fifty thousand berserkers ready to rain down hell upon the Red Sox.

No one in the room was talking about the A's, or about the game they'd just played, or about the minefield of a season they'd endured. Instead, through grins that looked a little like snarls, the Yanks said, *Bring it on, bitches.* "This is the series we've been waiting for — the one everyone's been waiting for!" yelled Betances over a deafening track by Drake. Even Boone, Mr. Circumspect, was caught up in the flow, crowing that his players were locked and loaded. "We know how good they are, and we'll have to play our best to beat 'em — but the guys in this room can't wait to get it done."

Meanwhile, the champagne continued flying after everyone was drenched. The target of each fresh downpour was Judge, the evening's standout hero. Manfully, he kept trying to field writers' questions because, even in celebration, that is who Judge is: a guy who calmly stands there and does his job. He talked about the crowd — "they were so loud tonight, I couldn't hear the end of the National Anthem" — but otherwise he turned around every query to praise the players beside him. They, in turn, doused him with sticky spray that was the surest expression of love. Ballplayers don't have words for certain things, and by things we mean, of course, feelings. They don't tell the guy at the center of a clubhouse that they adore and depend on him; that's what horseplay's for. In those champagne gushers, they spoke for themselves and all those fans by saying, after their fashion, *Thank you.*

11

ALDS: RUNNING INTO AN OCTOBER BUZZSAW

Despite the block of bars facing Fenway Park, there's something quaintly charming about a pregame Red Sox crowd. That great pedestrian mall formerly known as Yawkey Way (then-named for the arrant racist who owned the Boston franchise for four largely segregated decades) is practically a lawn party for visiting scholars when set against the vehemence of Yankee Stadium. Couples from New York City who catch the northbound Acela can freely browse the pubs in their Jeter apparel without being doused in Sam Adams, and strike up conversations with local patrons that don't become restagings of Bunker Hill. However you explain it, there's a period of communion before hostilities start, a jolly couple of hours in which the celebration of baseball prevails over parochial loutishness. There are no cops walking point here in tactical armor, no snarling German shepherds barely tethered by leashes, no stone-faced parking clerks passing mirrors under your car. If you wish to compare the cultures of these teams, here's a handy marker of their mind-sets. The Yankees treat their fans like sleeper cells, half-expecting to find a bomb strapped to their chest. The Sawx assume good conduct from their faithful and are rewarded for it before a game. It's truly a sight to see — given what that crowd *becomes* the moment the Red Sox starter takes the mound. At that point, God help the folks who wore their Stanton grays. Even in Boston, good fellowship has a sell-by date.

There's also something quaint, if markedly less charming, about playing an actual ball game here. The ballpark opened in 1912, when humans were apparently the height of Shetland ponies. You enter the visitors' clubhouse — and you feel like you're in Colonial Williamsburg. The dimensions are puny, an assault on evolution; you imagine the clubhouse guys drying jockstraps with a *paddle*. The visitors' quarters are a frat-house prank on the road team (and out-of-town writers) gone horribly wrong. The room is so cramped, you have to stick your bottom in Stanton's face just to ask Gleyber Torres a question. It's also a death trap waiting to happen: the doors are single-file in, single-file out. All you'd need is some crank yelling "Fire!" and half the team would be trampled underfoot. You're reminded of the overheated squalor in Boston Garden when the Knicks of the 1980s would go in to play the Celtics and drop seven pounds of water weight by halftime.

All in all, Fenway is a marvelous place — for a wrecking ball. History is one thing, but this park's something else. It's a snow globe draped in recent pennants.

The Yankees opened the ALDS with three thoughts firmly in mind. The first was that their team was better than its record and the Red Sox were worse than theirs. This wasn't, strictly speaking, a fresh idea: for a month, the Boston media had been openly theorizing that the Sox were paper tigers. With the pot-stirring hosts on WEEI leading the charge, the indictments ranged from the leakiness of Boston's pen to the defects in its four likely starters. Sure, the Sox had swept the Yankees here in August, then coasted the rest of the way home — but *those* Yanks were ciphers, pale substitutes for the beasts who'd show up, in ill humor, on October 5. With all that retrenched muscle in their right-handed lineup, they'd bash the Green Monster — and Boston's middle-innings guys — like so many dime-store piñatas. Or so went the story in a town that still behaves like it hasn't won a pennant since Babe Ruth's trade.

The Yankees' second thought: they had a Sox-killer in Happ, who would pitch game 1 (and 5, if the need arose). In his twenty-one starts against them over the course of twelve years, he'd stoned each version of Boston's lineup that he faced, baffling them with his snake-charmer fastball. He didn't have to be perfect now; he just had to be Happ, the guy who would give them five strong innings, then hand a lead off to Chad Green. It scarcely mattered that the Yanks were facing their own assassin in Chris Sale. Oft-injured and seldom-glimpsed in the second half of the season, Sale was, at best now, a ninety-pitch curio whom they'd see through by the top of the sixth. And then, at worst, it was bullpen versus bullpen, and the Yankees *loved* their chances in that matchup.

Then there was their third thought, the break-glass-in-case-of-fire clause: they were going against David Price in game 2. Somewhere in Christendom, there's a forensic pathologist who can explain Price's tragic Yankee-phobia. Against everyone else, the man is magic, a wizard with a biting cutter. Against New York, he's a nervous breakdown in progress, a wretch who probably sweats when he dreams pinstripes. The Yanks had high hopes that they could steal game 1, but knew for a *stone fact* they'd win game 2. And if they snuck out of Fenway up two games to none, they'd all but punch their tickets to the ALCS, given the way Severino had pitched against the A's. No less sweet, they'd take a leisurely leak on the records the Sox had set all season — and on the many pomps and splendors of their recent past.

Since 2004, when the Sox stormed back and stole that championship series from the Yanks, they, not New York, have been the class of the American League. Yes, the Yanks have won six divisional titles to five for the Red Sox through 2018. But the Sox have won three Series to the Yankees' one — and in the Bronx, it's strictly World Series or bust. If you doubt that, just walk the inner concourse of the Stadium, where, every ten feet, there's a poster-sized print of Yankees battery-mates embracing after the final out of Series clinchers. There's Yogi hugging Whitey, Thurman hugging Goose, Posada hugging Rivera, and on and on. Archaeologists of the future who unearth these ruins might be tempted to tell those couples: *Get a room!* But such are the stakes when you play for the New York Yankees: either deliver the goods or get erased altogether from the walls — and collective cortex — of the empire.

In summary, then, the Yankees had a certain big-armed swagger when they took the field in game 1. They'd gotten hot at the right time, had Judge back to midyear form, and were sending their best man to the mound.

Those sentiments lasted exactly twelve pitches.

Happ came out of the pen with his worst stuff of the year: his four-seamer was as flat as a rope-swing tire. Nine starts out of ten, he gets that strange little rise just as his fastball breaks the zone. Hitters see it clearly till they're into their swing; then the pitch just ups and disappears. But that night — nothing. It sat there belt-high, a 92-mile-an-hour gift to his hosts. Velocity wasn't the problem — *perceived* velocity was, the magic that high spin rates produce. Happ made forty-four pitches, his shortest start in ages: he got three swings-and-misses from Red Sox hitters. And still, he kept going to his bread-and-butter pitch. Neither his two-seam nor his slider were biting either.

He somehow struck out Betts, the leadoff hitter, but served a scorched single to Benintendi. Then Happ, who couldn't locate, lost Steve Pearce, the exact wrong guy to walk. In stepped Martinez, who straight owns the Yankees and has the title and registration to prove it. Happ fell behind him and threw another four-seamer, his thirteenth pitch of the night. Martinez clubbed it over the Monster like a nine-iron hit in anger, a blur that barely cleared the top of the wall. And that, essentially, was that for game 1. When Happ departed in the third with runners at the corners, Chad Green came on and fanned the flames. The guy with the best high fastball in their pen got beat around the hind parts by Pearce and Martinez and allowed both runners to score. It was a one-two punch the Yankees didn't see coming — and a combo from which they never really recovered.

Every quality team likes to think it has a formula, a pathway to pre-scriptive success. For the Yankees, that formula is power plus power: home run prowess paired with killer relievers. Other teams are happy if they have a single closer; in the playoffs, the Yanks had *five*. Here was a proof-point of Cashman's faith in pile-on talent: he'd overstocked his bullpen with playoff-proven arms in the belief that they'd be the difference in October. But he'd bolted that premise onto a shaky foundation: the conviction that his starters could go five innings against great lineups. And there, it turned out, he was badly wrong: those starters, Tanaka excepted, crapped out early. Three of the starts were so woefully brief that the Yanks' pen was never a factor in the series. Among them, Happ, Severino, and Sabathia pitched a total of eight innings, allowing fourteen runs and disarming their team before it had a chance to fight. They didn't throw strikes, couldn't put away hitters, and failed to contain the damage done with runners on. In Happ's case, failure was a harsh surprise. In Sevy's and CC's cases, it was not.

For much of the second half of the regular season, the team's youngest and oldest starters were basket cases. There's no point in piling on these poor souls again; their declines have been well documented already. The point, rather, is to acknowledge what both Boone and Cashman said at several points during the year: baseball will break your heart if you let it. For half the season, Sevy and CC were the Yankees' two best starters. One was the Cy Young favorite at the break, while the other looked like he could pitch for years and engrave his own bust in the Hall of Fame. Neither of them blew his arm out or was felled by a batted ball. Both simply stopped pitching well and never rebounded. With Sevy, it was youth that largely did him in. He lacked the guile and tradecraft to muddle through when his talent (and nerves) betrayed him. With CC, it was the reverse: all those thousands of innings and strikeouts had seemingly taken the last of his soft tissue.

There's little a team can do to gird for such a blow, unless it has the bankroll for six strong starters, one of whom it stashes for a rainy day. Some clubs do get lucky: that kid they're grooming at Triple-A suddenly comes of age and saves their season (cf. Walker Buehler with this year's Dodgers). Other teams — well, *one* team, the Houston Astros — are so skilled at acquiring and improving starters that they can prevail when a Dallas Keuchel has a down year. For everyone else, though, it's perniciously hard to keep a staff intact. Contenders like the Cards, who lost Carlos Martínez and Michael Wacha, the Diamondbacks (Robbie Ray and Taijuan Walker), and the A's (Sean Manaea, among many) might have made deep playoff runs had they not been bushwhacked during the year. It's cruel and inexplicable — and it happens all the time. Just ask that star-crossed bunch in Queens, who, for the last two years, watched their season's hopes blow up when young arm after young arm went down.

In the clubhouse after game 1, the Yankees were in shock. Though they'd made the score respectable by the end, the mood in the room harked back to August, when Sabathia got rocked in the series opener. Like CC, Happ had been taken apart by a prepared and patient lineup. Worse, their histories had been no help against a team that was vastly better than its past. Happ himself was helpless to explain his dreadful outing. He stood there manfully and answered each question ("I always stress trying to get strike one. I wasn't very good at that tonight, and the big hit cost me"), but he was as baffled by his dismantling as the players dressing beside him. Like so many of these Yankees, Happ's an honest and honorable man, a guy who, within the parameters of the sport, speaks to you from his heart. But what is there to say, finally, about the randomness of human performance? Prior to this game, he'd made three starts in his playoff life, one for the Phillies in 2009 and the other two — both of them solid — for Toronto. He'd also pitched splendidly down the stretch, been the Yankees' best starter for two months. Clearly, he was built for pressure games, but on this one pivotal night he didn't produce. Happ isn't Justin Verlander, who can skunk you with his curveball when his best pitch, the fastball, isn't clicking. That's why you pay up and don't think twice when a Verlander hits the market in July. Do you want to be the guys who broke the home run record for the season — or the ones carousing on the mound in all those posters on your walls?

There was a second fail in game 1 that shadowed game 2, and however many games stretched beyond it. Five times Stanton came up in key moments; four of those times he whiffed. The worst of his punch-outs came in the seventh, when the Yankees, down three, had the bases full and no one out and were facing a wobbly Matt Barnes. (Barnes had come on, thrown a wild pitch to Gardner, then walked him to load the bags.) Stanton had already K'ed twice with runner(s) aboard, so expectations were modest. All the Yankees hoped for was a medium fly ball that would score McCutchen and move Judge up to third. Instead, this is what they got: strike one, strike two, a pair of waste pitches, then — for the nth time all year — a Stanton flail-and-miss on a curve away.

In Fenway, the press box is so high above the field that you can barely *see* the game, let alone hear it. But virtually audible from the back of that nosebleed room was the air going out of the Yankees' dugout. So often had Stanton mounted unproductive at-bats that this one could've (should've?) been assumed. But in his last plate appearance in the wild-card game, he'd crushed a hanging slider 440 feet to the bowels of the second deck — and given his teammates hope that they had him back. When Stanton is right, he *obliterates* mistakes, hitting balls so far and with so much force that they almost count for more than a single homer. Watch the way players in pinstripes react when Stanton does his number on a pitch. They jump and hop and dance jigs with each other, as if they've all done a vicious hit of nitrous. They can't help themselves: at some level, they're still just kids who stand in awe of the man. They also, frankly, love him — he's that unicorn superstar who works longer, harder hours than anyone else.

But the inverse is also true: when Stanton goes into slumps for long stretches, he seems to drain the lifeblood from this team. No one would accuse him of not working his tail off or of moping in the dugout during droughts. But when he's not on his game, there are downstream effects: the Yankees' offense seems to run out of gas. So it was in the divisional series: Stanton's four-for-eighteen — the four hits were all singles — delivered a gut-shot to his team's morale. Time after time, the guy who had carried the team when Judge was out failed with runners on, even in the one game that they won. (For the entire series, the Yankees scored fourteen runs; the Sox scored sixteen in *game 3*.) But the sad truth was that Stanton was going through a down cycle during the ALDS, and Yankee fans everywhere were feeling his immense frustration.

Not all of that lands on Stanton, of course. None of the Yankee hitters produced runs except for Judge and, for one rare game, Gary Sánchez. Otherwise, the lineup that terrorized the league looked terrified at the plate. It batted .214 and was even worse against anyone not named Price. The rest of the Sox starters cruised through their outings, particularly Eovaldi and Porcello, who couldn't be touched. In their moment of truth, the Yankees made Eovaldi into the second coming of Clemens and Rick Porcello (4.26 lifetime ERA) the spitting image of Greg Maddux.

But the biggest surprise of the divisional series was the efficiency of Boston's pen. All those leaky vessels — Heath Hembree, Ryan Brasier, Joe Kelly, Matt Barnes — were watertight with games on the line. Overall, the Sox middle men pitched nine and two-thirds innings, surrendered zero runs (earned or otherwise), and gave up a grand total of *one hit.* Their Yankee counterparts — Dave Robertson, Zach Britton, Chad Green, and Dellin Betances — posted solid but not shutdown numbers: 13.2 innings pitched, ten hits allowed, and three runs, each of them earned. And when it mattered most, their short men blinked. Green let both of his inherited runners score in the game 1 loss (5–4), and Britton served up the back-breaking homer to Christian Vázquez in the game 4 clincher (4–3). To be clear, then: the loss of this series was a team effort by the Yankees. The lineup, the starters, *and* the bullpen failed. Justice was served, the better team won — and as the old ball coach Bill Parcells used to say, *It wasn't even close for second.*

There isn't much point in reviewing the two losses after the Yanks tied the series at 1–1 — and even less to gain from rehearsing game 2, when they beat around Price, as expected. Still, there were several moments worth reviving here for what they said, in requiem, about this group.

The Yanks returned to the Bronx to play game 3 having wildly misread the meaning of game 2. To a man, they thought that *that* win was the truth and the loss in game 1 was an illusion. You could see it and hear it at 5:00 p.m., in their swaggering preparations in the cage. Judge and Stanton were hitting bomb after bomb, to the relaxed amusement of their mates, while Boone and his coaches were laughing and joking as they watched the guys get ready. In banter and body language, both players and coaches behaved like this was a rivalry game — in *April.* Veteran writers gathered behind the ropes near the dugout kept remarking how loosey-goosey the team looked. Not that their word is gospel, but good beat writers can always tell you the emotional weather of a club. Think of them as cops driving patrol in their cruisers while scanning the demeanor of corner boys. They know the whole story without stopping the car: who's slinging, who's holding, and who's packing the flamer. It's the nature of their job and they've done it forever, so they get the cues. Thus, too, the guys scribbling notes in their head while watching the Yankees work out. Here was a team that, by every indication, believed that it would sweep at home and go straight to Houston.

If reporters needed to corroborate what their eyes were seeing, they got it at 7:32. Severino, who said he always throws a ten-minute bull-pen, was still long-tossing off flat ground. That would've been fine if the game started at eight — but *first pitch was at 7:42.* Ron Darling, the ex-Met working the broadcast for TBS, astutely noted that Sevy hadn't warmed up yet and had just been told the start time by his pitching coach, Larry Rothschild. The kid scrambled to the pen, got *maybe* seven minutes in — and was a helpless mess from the moment he took the mound. That electric fastball he'd thrown in the wild-card game was nowhere to be found in game 3.

Straight from the gate, the Red Sox jumped him, hammering rockets to the gap in left-center. Gardner managed to run down all three ropes — but if ever a pitcher deserved to be pulled from a game after a one-two-three first inning, here he was. In the biggest start of his life, Sevy had virtually nothing.

But this wasn't about being young and not up to the job; that stuff you can, and should, accept. It was about undermining your talent, and your teammates' chances, with the whole season hanging on the line. We'll probably never hear from him what happened that night. In the clubhouse after the game, he spat on the idea that he'd done anything wrong (or different). "Who's *that* guy?" he snapped, referring to Ron Darling when reporters pressed the issue after the game. "How would he know what time I go out there? I came out twenty minutes before, like I always do." He also denied having less than ten minutes to warm up, though the TBS tape showed he hadn't. All Sevy's denial did was escalate the matter and further incense the millions who were already angry. YES's studio analyst, the typically diplomatic John Flaherty, shredded Severino on the postgame show. "There is *no* way you can go on a big league bullpen mound eight minutes before the scheduled first pitch and expect to be ready."

How stunning was that takedown? The YES Network subsequently fed that quote to all the media outlets, making it the unofficial position statement of the New York Yankees.

For one night, then, the ghost of Big Stein walked — but that's what happens when a good team goes to pieces. It absorbs the worst loss of its postseason life, a history dating back to 1901. It goes down by ten runs early, never utters a peep on offense, and sends its fans racing for the exits. "So awful," in Boone's words, was the 16–1 thrashing that the Stadium was half-empty by the sixth. Far beyond the walls of the big ballpark, the Major Deegan was slammed, one long snarl of departing traffic. By the time Austin Romine came out to pitch mop-up, there was no one in the seats *or* the streets. Even the cops had gone home to their wives and kids, or wherever it is they go after a tour.

All that remained was the formality of game 4. The Yanks, to a man, knew they were cooked as they somberly dressed after game 3. They stood and answered questions till the writers were gone, because no one on these Yankees runs and hides. But what was there to say? They'd had the crap kicked out of them — and the hard fact kicked in that the Sox were better. It was a tough nut to swallow after a year of believing that *they* were the gods' anointed. If you rewound the tape to winter — specifically, the day they traded for Stanton — the master narrative among these Yankees was that the dynasty was back. They weren't just big and bruising: they were baseball's version of the Hulk. With their height and heft and superhuman strength, they were the evolution in the on-deck circle, the forebears of baseball's mutant race. They'd turn the regular season into a video game, scoring runs by the bunches, hitting homers to Altair 3, and inflicting harsh justice on hanging curves.

And they'd do this with a smile, saving the planet and their sport, while waiting for the Marvel movie to come out. You could almost see it now: *BronxBombers Versus BoSox: Revenge of the Empire, Part VI*. To quote a narcissist ex-receiver who richly deserves to go nameless: *Better getcha popcorn ready, folks.*

And now? Precisely none of that would happen. No dog-pile on the mound after they beat the LA Dodgers; no ticker-tape procession down the Canyon of Heroes; no raucous team appearance on *Jimmy Fallon*. You could see that it hurt like hell, even as it was sinking in. The future of baseball wasn't theirs (not yet at least). Turns out you *can't* just hit the ball farther than other humans and expect the sport to fall down on its knees. You need to be able to shut down other good lineups, and to do so when the chips are on the line. You need to be able to score when you're not hitting for power, win games with variety as well as brawn. You need to be adept at some of the unsexy stuff: taking the extra base, bunting the ball past the pitcher, hitting it through the gaping hole at short. In short, you need to be more like the Sox and less like the X-Men, because baseball isn't a comic book anymore.

Ever since the sport clamped down on performance-enhancing drugs (PEDs) — suspending players half a season for one blown test and a full season (or more) for further offenses — teams have moved away from overdeveloped sluggers who hit homers but do little else to help. Between the end of this season and the start of the next one, there will be thousands of column inches spent on what the Sox did right and what the Yanks did wrong in 2018. Here's some free advice: save your breath, baseball sages. The difference between these teams can be summed up in one sentence: the Red Sox signed J. D. Martinez, and the Yankees dealt for Stanton. Put Martinez, that resourceful, run-producing genius, in the three-hole behind Hicks and Judge and watch the parade of big innings and early blowouts. Now slot Stanton after Betts and Benintendi and see how many of those five-run rallies never happen. Strikeouts aren't the cost of doing business in this game: they're the margin of error between a championship team and one that bows out early.

Now, to be fair to Stanton, he played the second half of the season with a tight hamstring that never loosened up. How much that hindered his stride and weight shift, no one seems to know. (The Yankees wouldn't say, and neither would Stanton.) To his sizable credit as both a man and a teammate, he showed up every day, played 158 games, and refused to sit out when the Yanks were banged up, soldiering on all summer. It must further be acknowledged that the Yanks won a hundred games, and that they did so while riding two keystone rookies who weren't quite ready for October. Gleyber Torres and Miggy Andújar are big stars in the making. Both are mortal locks to contend for batting titles and to be as potent as Betts and Bogaerts with some seasoning.

Indeed, the case can be made that these Yankees were *ahead* of schedule. For years, all anyone has talked about is the 2019 season, when, fortified by some combo of Machado-Harper-Kershaw, the Yankees will sail straight on to the World Series. And well they still might without *any* of those players — we can officially count out Kershaw, since he has re-upped with the Dodgers — and with only half a season, tops, from Didi Gregorius, whose elbow tear in the ALDS will cost him three or four months in 2019. It's entirely possible that, with the acquisition of James Paxton in November and the signing of a second starter (Happ? Patrick Corbin?), the Yanks can win the division next year and power their way to a pennant.

But it's just as feasible that their baked-in weakness will leave them short again. Unproductive at-bats with runners on base crippled the team all season. Yes, they were out-everything-ed by the Sox — but lest you forget, two of those four games were winnable one-run losses. What if Stanton *hadn't* struck out with the bags full in game 1, or whiffed with two aboard and no one out in the ninth inning of game 4? We'll never know, of course, but the sample size will grow; these Yankees will be in the playoffs for years to come. Will Sánchez figure out what he was doing wrong at the plate and regain his stature as one of the game's more feared hitters? Does Stanton, who's signed for nine more seasons at a pricey $240 million, come in next spring as a more disciplined hitter, one really ready to hit the ball where it's pitched? Will he discover a more consistent approach at the plate and recapture the kind of production he had when he was the National League MVP?

Or does he stand on his brand as a one-man wrecking crew and dare the fans, and the media, to come after him? Because, as day follows night, there'll be hell to pay if he has a couple more postseasons like this one. This town isn't Miami, and those folks in the stands aren't kindly old widows and snow-bird golfers. Just ask Alex Rodríguez what life can be like when the crowd turns against you in the Bronx.

Big Stein had it wrong, you see: This town doesn't love stars. It only loves the ones who actually deliver.

Some playoff losses hurt worse than others. After the Yankees' game 5 heartbreak against the Seattle Mariners in the '95 ALDS, their then-manager, Buck Showalter, wept quietly in his office. George Steinbrenner had stormed down into the clubhouse to blast him for blowing a two-games-to-none lead. But when he saw Showalter's head pressed against the desk, his shoulders heaving with sobs, Steinbrenner gently closed the door behind him and left the players to mediate their pain.

Then there was the fallout from this loss to the Sox, in which the response in the room was — roughly nothing. No tears or gnashed teeth, no brooding in stunned silence. Instead, what you heard was the rip-and-tear *krrrrrrich* of clubhouse guys taping up cartons. There used to be something called Garbage Bag Day, in which the players straggled in after a season-ending loss to collect their stuff and give a final comment. Not anymore, and certainly not this time. No one wanted to re-litigate what just happened. The better team had won — end of story.

"What a year they had — congrats to them," said a somber (but not morose) Aaron Judge. He didn't get an argument from the guys around him. In tone and in spirit, the clubhouse felt like the last day of a community college school year. There were a few meaningful hugs: Judge saying good-bye to Luke Voit; CC wishing Gray a good winter. What you *didn't* hear was a single Yankee say, "We'll get those sonsofbitches next year." Instead, just two words: "next year."

One by one, they stopped to trade farewells with the writers with whom they'd spent the last half-year. Happ stuck around to give his number to reporters, who'd be calling to check on his contract talks. "I was praying for another shot in game 5," he said, but that would have to wait till next October. Someone mentioned that the Yanks would be smart to sign him fast. "That would be nice," he said, and quietly slipped away.

As for Boone, he waited for most of the press to clear out, then toured the locker room to hug his players. "See you in a couple months," he said to Stanton. Stanton gave a pained smile that said, *I'm sorry.* There were more such exchanges as Boone made his rounds: an embrace and a couple of mumbled words. The last Yankee to leave was Sabathia. He stood before his cubby, signed a pair of new cleats, then placed them in Sonny Gray's locker.

Epilogue
NOVEMBER 2018

After a season ends, Yankee Stadium is a graveyard, or must surely feel like one to some of its neighbors. For five months, it looms there, darkly, in their midst, sending out nothing but ghostly emanations of the season, or seasons, past. Only the employee gate, at the butt end of the ballpark, stays open during the winter. After the early-morning arrivals of Cashman and his staff, nothing stirs there except Jerome Avenue stragglers en route to the IRT. In a community so reliant on the fortunes of the team for the jobs and retail traffic it provides, there is, in its annual closing, something distinctly funereal, as if the whole 'hood has entered a state of grief.

The morning we met with Cashman — five days after the loss to Boston — was appropriately wreathed in drab. A gray, steady rain, blown by fits and starts of wind, surged as press cards were presented to the guard. But once upstairs, in the executive suites on the second floor of the building, there was no sign of sadness or obsolescence. The band was back together as if it had never broken up: quants and scouts and senior vice presidents bustled past on their way to meetings. If anyone was still in mourning, it wasn't evident in their bearing. Instead, what they gave off was the usual beehive buzz. It was just another Monday at the office.

Cashman had been at his desk for hours already, but he wasn't working furiously on redemption. Instead, he was doing what he always does: talking on his overburdened phones. Let other general managers take golf vacations or go fly-fishing with their kids; Cashman, the grinder, was plugging away at his weeks-long list of calls. After the season ends, he begins his ritualized version of baseball's mating dance. He rings every other executive in the game and asks them what they're looking to do that winter. "Are they trying to move salary while adding a bullpen arm? Maybe there's a matchup down the road that works for both of us." By the end of the World Series, he's already finished doing recon on who's available, for what, on thirty teams (including his own). That isn't, for Cashman, a laborious drill: he *lives* for these weeks and stopless conversations.

How comfortable is Cashman with who he is and what he does? He greeted us wearing a French naval sweater that — *pourquois pas?* — had a hood attached. It says that he's fifty-one in the team's media guide, but the only indicator that the guy is middle-aged is the grudging surrender of his hairline. He never stops churning or lets his battery recharge, which is why he'll hold this seat till the day he keels over — presumably at his desk, returning a call. Nowhere in sports is there a more entrenched executive: Cashman is arguably the most powerful chief in baseball because he loves — and is loved by — this franchise. He has never presided over a losing season and never had to dismantle a broken roster and build a new one from scratch. Along the way, he has helped make the Steinbrenners unimaginable sums of money while doing very nicely for himself.

Men with his kind of clout usually want something in return: a percentage of the team, say, and the cover of *Sports Illustrated*. But Cashman still conducts himself like the kid he surely was when he reluctantly took the job in '98: as if he's hanging on by the skin of his teeth. Maybe it's just what happens when you've worked for Big Stein — your central nervous system never fully resets. Somewhere in your subconscious you still worry that the phone will ring and, when you answer it, screaming will commence.

What we learned in our final sit-down was that Cashman was done with 2018 and would spend zero time reviewing the tape. "We were good enough to win, but Boston played its 'A' game and we didn't," he said. He waited a beat, then gave an open-palm shrug whose meaning was, *What, me worry?* "Now, does that make the season a failure? Objectively, no. We won nine more games than we did last year and broke the home run record. But we missed an opportunity with a very talented team, and there's no second chances or looking back. The season's over, and now we're trying to figure out how to make what we have better."

He acknowledged the failures of several stars in the playoffs, Stanton, Sánchez, and Sevy chief among them. "G did everything we asked of him, outside of perform when it counted, but when he's on, he's unstoppable. And then, when he's off, he's so off, it's horrific — swinging at a curve seven feet in front of the plate. But, I mean, he's one of the better players in the game today. He just happened to get off track at the wrong time."

It's a reasonable view of Stanton, one echoed by Cashman's peers. "He's a certain type of hitter, and what he does, he does well," said Billy Beane, speaking of Stanton after the ALDS. "He's not Miguel Cabrera, but who is? He's going to hit thirty to forty homers and drive in a hundred in an average season, and there's tremendous value in that." Still, Cashman was pressed about Stanton's yearlong lapses with runners in scoring position and reminded that Stanton had spent a month in Tampa working specifically on his stroke to right. "Well, *all* these guys have characteristics of hitting to right, and without question, we preach using the whole field. But when someone goes out there and wants to do damage, they can get ahead of themselves."

Apropos of that, he added: "I don't think Gary Sánchez was trying to pull as much as he did, but in the second half, he lost confidence. So now we have to try and get him untracked, be the kraken he was for two years."

Of Severino's downturn, Cashman was somewhat sharper. "He was tipping pitches," he said bluntly. "You give these hitters a chance to know what's coming, and they're going to hurt you till you fix it." How did teams discover what Sevy's tells were? "Well, there's so much video out there—once one team spots it, it spreads like wildfire. Not saying the Red Sox told *everybody*, but that's how it works in the division. You've got a buddy in Toronto, you say, 'This is what we've got, now go out and whack the guy.'" The tipping, he said, was solvable, but not during the season, "when you'd have to take him offline for three weeks." That's what the off-season and spring would be for: restoring Severino to "a frontline starter, not the end-of-rotation guy he became."

And so it went for a lively couple of hours as Cashman stood firm that his team had the goods and would bust its tail making those goods better. Regarding "Miggy and Gleyber expanding the zone" down the stretch and "showing some warts on defense," the solution was to "get out the Compound W [over the winter] and get rid of those." Both were "high-ceiling guys" whose growth would boost the lineup, as would the return of Clint Frazier, "an A-level talent" who could be a star in left, assuming he was past his concussion problems. Cashman was proud to have added a guy like Voit to the "talent matrix" and said he'd go into Tampa as the presumptive starter at first. He also heaped praise on McCutchen and Britton, both of whom he'd clearly re-sign if talks with their people worked out. But no less clear was Cashman's hunger for more—"more talent, more leadership, more everything"—as he trawled the winter market. "Remember: we won 125 games in '98, then went out and traded for Clemens. Same thing now: we're not sitting back. We want to push deep into October."

About the futures of Gardy and CC, Cashman wouldn't comment, even to speculate off the record. The team's organizational meetings were to be held in a week, and he wasn't about to tip his hand on decisions the assembled brass would make. (As it turned out, Gardner and Sabathia both re-signed for one year, the opening volleys of what would surely be a busy and noisy winter.) Indeed, if any news emerged from our final meeting, it concerned the power of the quants. Per Cashman's directive, that department had equal say when it came to roster additions and subtractions. He even hinted that the quants could *overrule* him about player acquisitions. When the list of prominent free agents was put in front of him, Cashman gave an unprintable pan to several names at the top. "I don't like his act — *at all,*" he said of one of them. Of another, he jeered, "He takes games off. You could tell in the first at-bat if he showed up."

However, "the analytics guys will have a different position because they're sharks," he went on. "They swim, they feed, they have no emotion. Is a guy better than what we have now? Then they're in." If Cashman ever expected to have his opinions echoed by the quant staff he created, he'd certainly been disabused of it by now. "Their thing is, hey, that fish has swum beside me for the last five miles and he's my buddy and stuff, but right now, I'm hungry, so fuck him." In short, the numbers do all the talking at the Yankees' year-end meetings. Cashman's reluctance notwithstanding, the quants (and Hal Steinbrenner) would dictate whether the team signed a max free agent. Fiscal restraint only gets you so far when you share a division with the spendthrift Red Sox.

In the end, Cashman wrestled us to a draw regarding his take on the season he'd just wrapped. He wouldn't call it a disappointment, nor a cause for cheer, perhaps because he felt both emotions acutely. Or maybe he was telling the truth when he said that he "didn't get emotional because it's my job *not* to anymore. When you have a chair like I have, there's an understanding that comes over time." There were seasons when "we overperformed, like 1996, when we beat the Braves," and other seasons when the Yanks were the darlings of Vegas and crapped out in four games. Still, it was hard to imagine *not* having your heart broken, after working so hard for so long. Maybe the fairest read was that, whatever he actually felt, Cashman wasn't going to say it for public consumption.

If he's had it with any aspect of his job, it's the deathless media scrutiny of his moves. He refers to the hot-take spins as "narratives," as in "the narrative we strike out too much. Well, we *didn't* strike our way out of the Boston series. We hit too many grounders, which is unusual for us. We normally hit in the air and over the fence." After twenty years, such irritants still get under his skin, in part because it's a fight he'll never win. He works in a city with two watch-dog dailies and a pair of sports-talk stations that do not sleep. At any hour, day and night, someone's second-guessing his judgment — and his judgment is the thing for which he's prized. He has troves of information that New York sportswriters and bloggers know absolutely nothing of, dozens of staffers spitting out data on decision-points, and an owner whose long-term financial agenda has ruled out some big deals. Still, outsiders depict Cash as the man with the golden calf, able to buy a superteam at a moment's notice. That stuff got old for him a long time ago — specifically, back when it was true. All George's star-searching ever accomplished was to block the *next* dynasty from being launched.

Cashman won that fight, and virtually all of the fights since, because his vision was simply better than everyone else's. The basis of his big idea: spend on hard goods, not soft ones — on structure, scouting, player development, and analytics. There's something humble in his construct: it acknowledges the human limits of even the most brilliant athletes. For the cost of one A-Rod, you can build academies in countries that will send you Gleyber Torreses by the bushel. Instead of Yoenis Céspedes, you can staff up strong in Tampa and spoon-feed all those kids in your Rookie Leagues. In short, you do best by doing all the right things, not just for your team but for your culture. You assemble a staff that works investment-banker hours and sweats each detail of the job. You sink resources into the assets that matter most: talent, character, supply chain. You promote those people who tell the truth to each other in the service of your product. And yes, you sell that product at an absolute premium and make no apologies for the markup. Quality costs more, and there's a reason for that: it holds up its end over time. You want a Hermès bag, it'll run you five grand — but you'll pass it down to your daughter. You'd rather pay $250 for the Michael Kors knockoff? You'll pass it to Goodwill in two seasons.

Because that's, essentially, what Cashman and Co. peddle: a luxury brand that happens to be a ball club. What its millions of fans buy is a marquee of sustained excellence and a franchise that stands by its word. To be sure, people bitch about the price of Legends seats. But it's probably a good bet that the people bitching loudest aren't Yankee fans. For them, the money spent brings a sure return: seven months of crackling entertainment. They get good-guy protagonists like Judge and Didi to play their hearts out every day and never betray them. They get wunderkind rookies every spring to fall in love with as the season progresses. And they get a management staff that swings for the fences whenever the trade deadlines roll around.

In sum, then, full marks go to Cashman and his owner for crafting a team that lives up to its legend. Twenty years ago, Cash was made first mate on the *Queen Mary* and managed to keep the old girl shipshape. When at last he got the boat under his own command, he swapped it for one of those super-yachts with Rolls-Royce engines and a helipad. It's lean, it's mean, and it'll get you where you're going in the style to which you've grown accustomed. But — and there is always a *but* in this world — Cash knows just one way to travel. For the best part of a century, his team has stood for power, in all its brute expressions. Star power, slugging power, the power of the checkbook — power is what the Yanks do *because they've always done it.*

But power at the expense of everything else is a trap they've set for themselves. This team's so overleveraged on one-trick sluggers that it has no option when they swing and miss. These Yankees don't win, not because they can't run, but because they don't even bother pretending to try. The bunt, the steal, the extra base taken — all those are affronts to their self-conception. Never mind that the Core Four rosters won four rings by doing those things better than everyone else. The current-day Yanks have doubled down on their bet that the three-run homer conquers all. Let the Red Sox devote an entire field to the art of hitting with two strikes. (As *Sports Illustrated*'s Tom Verducci reported, the Sox set up a station to teach their players how to extend, prolong, and win at-bats in spring training. Cora, their manager, credited that drill for the team's move-the-line production.) Let the Sox purposely develop hitters who use *all* their tools to threaten and wear down pitchers, beginning with Betts, Benintendi, and Bogaerts. Let their manager have an inventory of cross-trained fielders he can plug in and play at several positions and starters who are game enough to come on in late innings and get three crucial outs in the World Series. The Sox are a team, and an organic culture, that gobbles up new ideas. If it's smart and it works, it goes straight into the mix, and who cares if it isn't on brand?

Early on in Cashman's tenure, the Yankees fielded teams that were good enough to win rings but didn't. Those groups that fell short from '01 to '07 might serve as an object lesson. You can put together a roster that has everything — except the extra gear today's Red Sox have. Cashman has built a club that will win a boatload of games over the course of the next ten years. It's young and it's vibrant and has talent to burn — and that's precisely what will happen if things don't change. It takes courage to course-correct when you're damn good already and making money hand over fist. It takes even more nerve to admit to yourself that your archrival does it better. But Cashman's been here before, and he's told himself that truth. The proof is in these next-gen Yankees.

As our final meeting ended, he said something instructive that he'd do well to take to heart. "I don't want to be talking in some article twenty years from now about the Yankees team that broke the home run record, *but* . . . We play for one thing, and that's to win in October. We had the opportunity this year, but just . . . didn't."

If he really means those words, then surely there's a field on a back lot in Tampa he can designate for two-strike hitting drills. It wouldn't take much in terms of capital outlay: a pitching machine you can dial up to 100, an assistant hitting coach to supervise the drills, and the humility to entertain a new idea — even if it came from those cursed Sawx.

Bob Klapisch
Paul Solotaroff
December 1, 2018

An Afterword on the 2019 Season

The summer of 2019 flipped the script, telling a story of spunk and perseverance. The Yanks ran away with the American League East, sprinting from the gate in a wire-to-wire job despite horse after horse going down. Judge, Stanton, Didi, Sevvy, Andujar, Betances, Sanchez, Hicks — on and on till they ran out of stars and a bunch of nobodies was summoned. Gio Urshela, Mike Ford, Cameron Maybin, Mike Tauchman: the B-Team Bombers showed up and showed out, doing the little things the big guys wouldn't. They hit behind the runner, took the extra base, and played their hearts out off the bench when the starting lineup finally got well again in August. The Yankees called their mojo "The Next Man Up." Another tissue tear or bone break? No problem, champ, we got you covered. With their *joie de vivre* and small-ball moxie, they seemed to hail from another age — specifically, the Core Four days. It was *fun* again to watch the Yankees; you never knew which role player would act the hero.

Their leader was the ultimate utility tool: DJ LeMahieu, also known as The Machine. All *he* did was everything: hit for average, drive in runs, play each of the infield spots. The guy they brought over to be a deluxe spare part turned out to be the gamer who defined this bunch. In his willingness to do whatever Boone asked, DJ changed the team's ethos from bully-boy swagger to a grinder's grit. And *that*, more than homers or the team's return to health, augured well for an October run.

And so it was — at least in the ALDS, when the Yanks out-every-thinged the overmatched Twins and tooled up for Armageddon 2.0. As Judge himself had told us in a sit-down in August: "Us versus the Astros is gonna be the *real* World Series." At that stage, no one but the Dodgers would've squawked. Any dissenters in Washington, DC, were too far off the sonar to be heard. *No one* foresaw that Nationals' wave forming from the shoreline of midsummer. But the Astros' eventual takedown of the Yankees? Now that, to quote the great García Márquez, was a death foretold.

Brian Cashman took nearly a week after season's end to hold a post-mortem at the Stadium. Perhaps he spent those six days chanting in an ashram — or drinking himself blotto to salve the sting. When he appeared before a roomful of reporters at the press conference on October 29, he took their questions with a mortician's calm, breaking down the loss to the Astros in rigidly clinical terms. Though he admitted that the Yankees had failed — *again* — he insisted that 2019 "wasn't a failed season." In both message and demeanor, this didn't wear well with the fifty or so writers who'd shown up. For one thing, there wasn't even a hint of anguish in his droning dissection of the facts. No catch in his throat, no long breaths sighed out: you would have thought you were hearing from a harbormaster who'd just closed the marina for the winter. For beat guys who'd watched Mo Rivera go locker to locker, apologizing to each and every one of his teammates after blowing Game 7 of the 2001 World Series to the Diamondbacks, Cashman's sangfroid was not acceptable. Not this time, and certainly not against this rival. For the third year in four, the Astros had *owned* the Yankees, and the fans wanted tears, if not blood.

But Cashman proved again that he doesn't *do* suffering — at least, not for the delectation of the public. Grief, however muted, is an admission of something: failure, regret, the main chance missed. Cashman, per his custom, admitted to nothing; he's too stubborn even to concede the obvious. Here was a team that, for the first time since its birth, had failed to win a championship in the course of a calendar decade. And here was a team he had pushed all in on, unlike the group in 2017 and '18. He'd assembled the most expensive bullpen in the history of the game, and built a roster so deeply provisioned that it weathered plague-level injuries to win its division.

Here, if ever there was one, was a Cashman-made squad with the stuff for a World Series berth: a mix of stars and resourceful bench guys, of playoff-tested veterans and precocious kids, of mercenaries and homegrown talent. But in its six-game stall-out in the ALCS, his crew was sunk again by old flaws. It couldn't hit in key spots, or get length from its starters, or depend on its overexposed pen to pitch around late-game landmines. It failed, in short, the way it always has since Cashman redrew its blueprint: by relying on two strengths — power and the pen — to plug up gaping holes. Where the Astros and Nationals deployed the true formula — it takes *several* aces, not one, to win a ring now — Cashman plowed forward with none. That has gotten to be an old story quickly.

Cashman opened the presser with a medical report: imminent surgeries for Tanaka, Voit, and Hicks, none of whose injuries impacted the series or were major concerns going forward. Even the cleanup of Tanaka's elbow was a nonstory; he'd been brilliant in his game 1 outing against the 'Stros, allowing a single hit in a 7–0 win. Alas, he was far less so in his game 4 start, allowing three earned runs over five messy innings in a decisive 8–3 loss. The series wasn't lost yet; the end came two nights later, with a walk-off bomb by José Altuve at the hands of Aroldis Chapman. But in Tanaka's good/bad body of work hung the tale of this rotation. It was good enough to beat the likes of the Twins, but not nearly up to the patient 'Stros, who waited and waited for pitches they wanted and hit the homers that counted. More to the point, no one on this Yankees staff was named Verlander, Cole, or Greinke.

That was the sword that hung over Cashman: How could he call 2019 a success when the team that beat him had *all* those pitchers, in large part because he didn't get them? Nor, for that matter, had he gotten Patrick Corbin, choosing instead to re-up J. A. Happ, who'd been utterly useless all season. *That* was the question he was going to have to answer, once he got done with the M*A*S*H list.

WFAN's Sweeny Murti kicked off the brawl. "There are several starting pitchers over the last few years that you passed on that are in the World Series now . . ."

Cashman shot back aridly: "I *didn't* pass on them."

He promptly launched into his point-by-point rebuttal. Verlander went from the Tigers to the Astros because Hal wanted to get under the luxury salary cap. (Never mind that Cashman then traded for Stanton, queering his luxury-tax status for the next decade.) Cole went from Pittsburgh to Houston in 2018 because the Astros made a superior offer. (Never mind that the Pirates would have taken Clint Frazier and Miggy Andujar, two players without clear roles in 2020.) And the Nationals, per Cashman, had outbid him on Corbin, as if *that* settled the matter. No one in baseball has the Yankees' money or its overseas pipeline of kids. If Cashman properly valued elite starting pitching, one or more of those men would have been Yankees.

Murti went back at him, raising those points. Cashman returned fire with "facts." His team had won 103 games — up for the fifth year in a row — and captured its first division title in seven years despite a record number of stints on the injured list. Then he reached for his buzzword. "You don't get everything you want all the time," he said. "But I can sleep at night with the *process* we have in place. It's served us well to take a legitimate shot at the championship, despite some of the options that went elsewhere."

Presumably, none of his equivocations made the Yankees feel better. Boone, for one, hadn't watched a replay of Altuve's homer — and from the look of him as he sat and took questions at the presser, he probably never would. But at least he wasn't weeping, as Aaron Judge was in the aftermath of game 6. The air in that clubhouse was thick and damp, though you could still hear the air guns going off outside. They pumped out blue and orange confetti at the thousands of fans partying in their seats. You could also hear the ballpark's Home Run Train blast its horn every couple of seconds. The Yanks, meanwhile, sat stonefaced at their lockers, none of them speaking or packing. Only Boone seemed to be able to locate his voice. He circled the lockers, whispering into his players' ears. Judge hugged him and the teammates lockered nearest him, then turned his back on the cameras. If he hoped that no one would see him crying, his huge shoulders gave him away.

Finally, the undisputed leader of the clubhouse turned to deliver the truth. "No matter how many games we won, or whatever else we did, this season is a failure," Judge muttered. "We'll be thinking about this for a while. I'll be thinking about it all off-season. Every single day."

Bob Klapisch
Paul Solotaroff
November 1, 2019

Acknowledgments

No book of any heft or ambition is possible without those working behind the scenes.

We are deeply indebted to Rick Wolff, who steered this book with a steady hand and craftsman's grasp of the game; David Vigliano, who was responsible for finding a home for this book; Bruce Nichols, publisher of Houghton Mifflin Harcourt; David Eber, HMH's legal counsel; Megan Wilson, the gifted HMH publicist who kept the wraps on everything and then let the world know about the book in a big, big way; Hannah Harlow, who expertly oversaw the marketing and advertising campaign; Cindy Buck, the tireless copyeditor who, despite being a Red Sox fan, really came through in the clutch; Rosemary McGuinness, the trusty editorial assistant who kept all the moving parts in sync; the entire production crew at HMH, especially Chloe Foster, Laura Brady, Beth Burleigh Fuller, Lisa Glover, and Katie Kimmerer, who worked long hours to make sure the manuscript and photos got to the printer on time, and the entire HMH sales team for doing such a tremendous job in getting the book out to fans.

We also want to thank the Yankees' Brian Cashman, Randy Levine, and Hal Steinbrenner, who were so generous with their time and knowledge; Yankees PR guru Jason Zillo, who made us feel like insiders; Geoff and Jina Klapisch, whose home served as our Boston headquarters, and Ken Davidoff and Mike Vaccaro of the *New York Post,* our resident consiglieres.

Bob Klapisch
Paul Solotaroff

Sources

Take a look at any grainy, back-in-the-day photo of batting practice at Yankee Stadium. Chances are, you'll find a group of reporters hanging around the cage. The scene is pre-smartphones, pre–tape recorders, pre-Twitter, pre-Statcast — but the newsmen are practicing an art that technology will never replace: asking the next question, gathering panoramic intel, and reporting it to the reading public.

Much of modern sports journalism relies on data, and it's been a boon for millions of numbers-obsessed fans. Grantland Rice and Red Smith might or might not have embraced WAR and FIP — but their writing and reporting skills would've translated in today's culture. Then as now, deep reporting is king, and that's *Inside the Empire*'s coin of the realm: the kind of knowledge that only comes from earned access.

In writing this book, we spoke extensively to the most senior members of the Yankees organization, including owner Hal Steinbrenner; president Randy Levine; general manager Brian Cashman; chief operating officer Lonn Trost; department directors Mike Fishman, Damon Oppenheimer, Eric Schmitt, and Kevin Reese; manager Aaron Boone; and — of course — every player on the Yankees' active roster. We interviewed the team's scouts, minor league coaches, managers, and officials, player development gurus, and some of the prospects on the farm. We also talked with players from other big league ball clubs to get their perceptions of the Yankees. We reached out to industry stars like Billy Beane and Omar Minaya for their perspectives, and to other executives who chose to remain anonymous.

Similarly, while all the players were queried on the record, some asked to go nameless when sensitive subjects were broached. All of our many hundreds of interviews were recorded, either electronically or in writing.

One way or another, the reporting over the last nine months has been tireless, same as it ever was. We'd like to think that those old-school beat writers would've been proud.

Index

About the Authors

BOB KLAPISCH has covered baseball for the *New York Post, New York Daily News,* and *Bergen Record,* as well as ESPN, FOX Sports, and *USA Today.* His work has appeared in *Sports Illustrated, Rolling Stone,* and *Men's Journal.* Klapisch has won several Top Five awards in the prestigious Associated Press Sports Editors contest and appears regularly on MLB Network. A graduate of Columbia University, where he played varsity baseball, Klapisch continues to pitch in the semiprofessional Metropolitan League in Bergen County. He and his family live in Westwood, New Jersey.

PAUL SOLOTAROFF is a veteran feature writer at *Rolling Stone* and *Men's Journal.* An investigative journalist whose fixed beat is social justice, he helped break the NFL concussion scandal, reported the horror-show conditions at Walter Reed Hospital, and wrote a series of stories that helped free innocent men who were doing life without parole in state prisons. Winner of two Genesis Awards and a National Press Club Award, he is a Pulitzer Prize and National Magazine Award finalist, as well as the best-selling author of three previous books. He lives in Nyack, New York, with his wife, Cynthia, who leaves the room to preserve her hearing and dignity when he watches the Yankees.